Entertaining and Educating Young Children

Expert advice from:
Nicola Hall, BA, QTS

Cover design by
Mary Cartwright

Entertaining and Educating Young Children

Caroline Young

Illustrated by Shelagh McNicholas
and Ruth Russell

Designed by Ruth Russell
and Laura Hammonds

Edited by Felicity Brooks
and Emma Helbrough

American Editor: Carrie Armstrong
Cooking Consultant: Barbara Tricinella

Contents

Make, paint and draw

Music and songs

Make-believe

Books and stories

Letters and numbers

My world

The world around me

Active play

Food and cooking

Active minds

The screen scene

Trips and traveling

Time to celebrate

Useful information

Introduction

This book is full of activities and play ideas for young children. As anyone who takes care of children will know, they usually don't need much encouragement to play: whether it's with toys, with other children, on their own, or with you, they will be playing in some way for most of their waking hours.

Play is how children explore and investigate the world, and gradually gain an understanding of it. Your role as their caregiver is vital in making sure they get as many chances to learn through play as possible… and that's where this book will help you.

This book has lots of ideas for encouraging different types of play, including creative play...

What can I do?

Providing a child with lots of play opportunities may sound like hard work, but try to remember that what seems ordinary to you, such as a walk to the store, can be the day's most exciting event for a young child, if you help make it so. Children learn through everyday life, and its experiences – and for them, everything is new and exciting.

...role-play,

...and small world play.

Your role is vital in helping children to play and learn.

Ways of playing

Most children play naturally, with or without lots of encouragement or toys and by the time they are about two-and-a-half, they can play in several ways, each of which helps them learn and develop. Childcare experts describe the different ways of playing as solitary, parallel, associative or cooperative (see right and below). It's a good idea to try to make sure a child has chances to enjoy them all on as regular a basis as you can.

Many children enjoy playing by themselves for periods of time. This discovery time is described as solitary play.

Young children often play happily alongside another child or adult, but not with them. This is known as parallel play.

When children play with each other, sharing toys and working things out together, it is called associative play.

Older children may play games that need rules, or planning with other children. This is cooperative play.

What can play do?

Many children between two-and-a-half and five years old are also cared for outside the home. Professionals are trained to make sure the children learn, and develop, through play. They usually have lots of facilities and equipment to help them. You don't have to reproduce this at home, but you can offer many similar kinds of play and learning experiences. On the right are some of the things children will discover when you do.

- How other people feel
- How things work
- How to make things
- How to share with others
- How to show their ideas and feelings
- How to do new things
- How to follow rules

Getting the most from this book

The activities in this book are divided into themes, or kinds of play. None of them is expensive, or complicated. The main goal is for both of you to have fun. Keep in mind that every child is different and develops at a different rate, so you may find some ideas are more suitable than others for the child you're caring for.

You may also need to help more, make minor changes, or try another activity if they aren't interested. Children have likes and dislikes, just as adults do, and it's never a good idea to push a child to do something they're not ready to do. This will only frustrate them, making them less willing to try it again.

Provide the playthings and some ideas, but make sure children have time to play in their own way, too.

Useful tip

The development charts on pages 122–123 give more detail on when most children do what, but they are only guidelines, as every child is unique.

Make it a point to enjoy the time you spend with young children, as they gain more from it if you are all having fun.

Let young children find out by themselves the best way to do some things.

How much help?

As you try the ideas, you may need to offer more support to younger children, and less to older ones. However much you help, be careful not to direct their play too much. If you take over, they won't really be playing, or learning, anymore – so resist the urge to finish that block tower for them if you can.

Make, paint and draw

This part of the book is full of ideas that encourage children to try art activities, including drawing, painting, model-making and cutting and pasting. The goal is to let them see how much fun such creative play can be rather than to produce anything perfect, so relax, and enjoy yourselves.

Creative play

Children can express their feelings and ideas through creative play.

There is no right or wrong way to do things in creative play, which builds confidence.

They can learn about colors, shapes, different textures and materials.

They can paint and draw on their own, or with others.

Using different tools helps them master coordination skills.

Many three to four year-old children draw people like this, with stick arms and legs coming out of their heads.

You could tape a big piece of butcher paper to a wall with masking tape. Your child can draw on it whenever they want, creating their own mural.

Make your mark

Most young children don't need much encouragement to draw. Their excitement in realizing that they have drawn something just by moving a crayon across some paper will grow, too, as their pictures gradually become more sophisticated. What children draw can say more about the development of their thoughts and feelings than any other kind of play.

Holding steady

It takes children time to learn how to hold a pencil as adults do, in what is called the tripod grip, and this isn't something that can be hurried. If they are finding it tricky to hold and control crayons in this way, try buying triangular wax ones, or pen grips, specially designed to help. Don't worry if a child doesn't draw anything you can recognize. It's all about exploring what they can do, and enjoying trying things out at this stage. Remember to ask them what they are drawing and to praise whatever they produce.

Children need to know that it's fine to draw in some places, but not in others. If you can, make sure your child understands that paper and pens will always be available if they keep to this rule. You could set up a drawing area on a small table or on a plastic mat or on some paper on the floor.

What shall I draw?

Some children are bursting with inspiration about what to draw, but others need more help. Try offering coloring books, dot-to-dot pictures or printed patterns to color in. They'll still be learning how to control a crayon, choose colors and concentrate. You could let them see you drawing something, too, and try to guess what it is:

Many young children have a clear idea of what they want to draw, so leave them to it.

  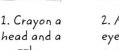

1. Crayon a head and a muzzle.

2. Add ears, eyes, a nose and a mouth.

3. Now give the bear a round body.

4. Add arms and legs and color it in.

As they progress, it is a good idea to begin encouraging children to try to copy what they see around them in their drawings. Called 'observational drawing', this activity helps children notice, understand and copy detail in what they see – all useful skills. Here's how to go about it.

Drawing equipment

• Build up a selection of drawing equipment. Most children find wax crayons or dustless chalks easiest to start with.

• If you buy markers, make sure they're non-toxic and washable. Get children into the habit of putting tops back on too.

• Computer paper, butcher paper and some food packaging make good drawing paper.

Choose an object with a clear shape, such as a flower or favorite toy and get the child ready to draw it.

Ask the child to look at whatever they are going to draw very carefully. Talk about its shape, colors and features. When you feel they have an idea of what to do, help them choose a starting point. Give them lots of encouragement as they try to get what they see down on paper.

Wax crayon projects

• Wax crayons work well on colored paper. Try bright colors on black paper for fireworks and white crayons on blue paper for clouds.

• Draw pictures with wax crayons and then paint over them with watery paint. The wax pictures will still be there.

• Crayoning onto some wax paper makes a picture you can stick onto a window and let the light shine through.

• Lay some paper over small, flat objects, such as coins, keys or leaves, and rub wax crayons over them to make patterns.

More to draw

As young children learn how to control pens and crayons, they will probably start to enjoy using different drawing effects in their pictures. Over the months, they may begin to think about their drawings more before they make a start, and produce more detailed pictures. The ideas on these pages will encourage children to experiment as they draw.

Wax works

Wax crayons are so adaptable that you may find young children happier to use them than colored pencils, which always seem to need sharpening. Many wax crayons end up snapped into pieces, but those pieces can still draw pictures. On the left are some mini-projects children can try with wax crayons.

Show children how to press wax crayons hard for denser colors, and more lightly for a softer effect.

Me

Mummy   Jessie

Small children often draw themselves as bigger than other family members at first.

Young children often want to draw pictures of themselves, or their families, but drawing people is tricky. Just let them enjoy trying things out and make sure you congratulate them for all their hard work. Try cutting a rough head shape out of paper, and letting your child draw on the face. Or the child could lie down and be drawn around, making a life-sized self-portrait to color in.

Follow the line

Some young children are not interested in drawing things they see, but just want to enjoy making marks on paper. Here are some ideas for letting them experiment and develop their control of pens and pencils:

• Lay some wax paper over a favorite picture or cartoon and let them trace over the lines.

• Let them 'take a line for a walk' all over some paper. They could color in the shapes they make afterwards.

• Make a pattern and then see if they can copy it. You could try spirals, stars or circles inside each other.

Useful tip

Plastic binders are useful for storing paper and artwork on art trips, especially if there's a chance of rain.

Art on the move

Drawing is an activity that's easy to do outside. You could just take a firm pad of paper, some drawing pencils and go out together to see what you can find to sketch. If you take a magnifying glass as well, you might find some bugs, flowers or leaves to look at in detail, and then draw.

If you're going out to draw, pack a simple children's art bag, including a pad of paper.

Talk about the features of things children draw, such as lines on leaves or the number of legs on animals.

You can buy ready-mixed children's paint in squeezable bottles.

Let's paint

It may seem as if you spend more time preparing and clearing up after a painting session than children spend actually painting, but it's definitely worthwhile because painting is one of the activities most young children want to return to again and again. The main equipment you need to start painting with young children is some non-toxic, washable paint and some paper. It's inevitable that there will be spills and smears, so it's a good idea to make the preparations on the left before you get started.

Getting ready

1. Protect the child's clothes from paint with an apron or one of your old shirts or T-shirts.

2. Cover the table they are going to paint at with a plastic tablecloth or some newspaper.

3. Covering any nearby floor or carpet with newspaper or a plastic sheet is also a good idea.

4. You could invest in some spill-proof paint containers. Most toy and craft stores sell them.

5. Have a damp cloth and water nearby in case paint gets spilled or hands need wiping.

Plastic egg carton

Many children prefer to paint with their fingers at first.

Paper plate

Useful tip

Don't forget that, if the weather's fine, you can set up painting outside, where mess doesn't matter so much...

Choosing paints and pots

The best paint to use with young children is ready-mixed, in bottles or pots. This is ideal for finger painting, too, as it's usually thick. If you feel paint needs to be thicker to avoid drips, you could stir a spoonful of flour into it. If you don't have paint pots, deep plastic jar lids, old muffin baking trays, styrofoam egg cartons or even paper plates make good paint holders, and keep the colors separate.

Brushes and paper

Somewhere around age three, most children can hold and control a paintbrush, and are ready to do so. There are lots of children's brushes to choose from, but it's best to start off with chunky ones, trying finer ones later. It's a good idea to buy quite a few, as children tend to mix colors by using the same brush for each one, producing endless 'brown' pictures. Supply a brush for each color, and explain why pictures may be clearer if colors are kept separate.

Large sheets of paper are best, as young children find it difficult to keep things small when they paint.

Useful tip

If you can, tape or pin a large piece of paper to a fence or wall outside, so children can really try out different brushes and colors.

More painting tools

For young children, finding out what paint can do is much more fun than producing a picture of something recognizable. Try these ways of painting with everyday things, which create some very different effects on paper. It may help if you show children what to do first, but most will soon have plenty of ideas of their own.

Pieces of sponge are easy to grip and can produce some satisfying results.

Cotton balls dipped in paint are good for pressing and dragging on paper. Try squeezing them into different shapes.

Pour paint into the middle of the paper and show how to blow it around with a straw. Make sure children don't suck.

Paint some blobs, press some clingfilm over the top and watch the blobs merge. Lift it off to reveal the picture.

More fun with paint

Once children have been given the chance to experiment with paint in their own way, many will be interested in doing more. Their ability to follow a series of steps will gradually increase, which makes it easier to try simple activities such as the ones shown here.

Making rainbows

Young children are fascinated when rainbows appear in the sky, on bubbles in the bathtub, or in the watery spray made by a garden hose on a sunny day. To paint a rainbow, line the paint pots up in order, and together follow the steps below. (See if they can figure out which color comes next each time.)

Red   Orange   Yellow   Green   Blue   Purple

1. Use a chunky brush for each color, or cut six brush-length strips of thin cardboard 2 inches wide.

2. Dip a brush or the end of a cardboard strip into each color and make arches on paper.

3. Keep going with all the colors until you have six arches, making a complete rainbow.

Letting children experiment with paint helps them gain confidence to start developing their own ideas. Once they have made a few rainbows, you could suggest they press their hands onto the paint (while it's wet) and then make rainbow handprints. They could stir a little craft glue and some glitter, sugar or play sand into the paint to add texture, or try the tracks idea on the left.

Useful tip

If you don't have any purple paint, just mix some red and blue paint together.

Track pictures

1. Ask the child to find a toy car or a doll (make sure they're washable).

2. Let them dip the car's wheels or the doll's feet into some pots of paint.

3. Now let them make colorful prints and tracks across a big sheet of paper.

Doll

Car tracks

Keeping artwork

Young children can produce a lot of paintings. Keeping them all may be impossible, but it's important for your child to know that you value what they have created. Here are some ways to make their paintings last a while longer:

• Choose an area to display paintings. The doors of cabinets and refrigerators are ideal. Change the pictures in this gallery regularly.

• Hang a line of string across a wall in children's rooms, so they can clip on their own paintings. (Make sure it's low enough for them to reach.)

• Take digital pictures of favorite paintings, drawings and models and store them on a computer. You could use one as your desktop wallpaper.

As a treat, buy a plain T-shirt and some fabric paints and let your child experiment.

Famous artists

It's never too soon to show young children paintings by famous artists. For a child, they are just pictures in which they do, or don't, like what the artist has done – it's as simple as that. You could borrow art books from a library so you can look at and talk about the paintings together. Children may want to try to copy the effects themselves.

Useful tip

Many children enjoy using simple computer art programs such as Paint from Microsoft® Windows® to make pictures, cards and party invitations.

A child's computer and wax-crayon picture based on the painting 'Squares and concentric circles' by Russian painter Wassily Kandinsky

A young child's 'Seurat' picture done with lots of dots of paint

1. Carefully fold a sheet of non-shiny drawing paper in half. Then open it out flat again.

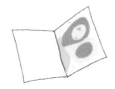

2. Let the child paint on one half of the paper. Try a simple pattern, or half a butterfly design.

3. Immediately fold the two paper halves together and press. Open it up again to reveal a complete picture.

Printing and patterns

Many young children enjoy printing and making patterns because they can produce big, satisfying pictures quickly. Printing encourages their creativity and can help them learn about different materials, textures, shapes and colors. On the left is one simple idea, but the main goal is to let children enjoy experimenting.

Making stamps

The idea behind printing is that whatever you press onto the paper leaves an impression. Sets of rubber stamps are great for young children to start printing with, but you can also use everyday objects, such as those listed below on the left. Printing with objects works best with thick paint; powder paint mixed with water is ideal. If you only have ready-mixed paint and the prints seem runny, stir in some flour as a thickener.

1. Pour a little thick paint into a saucer or into another shallow, flat container.

2. You could press a piece of thin kitchen sponge into the paint to make a print pad.

3. Show your child how to press an object into the paint or print pad, then onto paper.

Everyday objects to try printing with:

• Cardboard tubes
• Pasta shapes
• Toy blocks
• Cookie cutters
• Household string
• Bubble wrap
• Small sponges
• Halved potatoes
• Halved onions
• Leaves

Potatoes, cut in half and carved into a shape, make good, clear prints.

Handprints and footprints

If you have, or can create, a space where mess won't matter too much, let children make prints with their hands or feet. They may like the feel of paint between their toes, but even making prints with water is fun.

Print projects

• Outdoors, let children dip their bare feet into a shallow tray of paint, then walk all over a big sheet of paper.

• Make handprints every few months and look at them together to see how the child is growing.

• Cover fingertips with paint and look at the patterns in the skin before making prints of them.

Making patterns

Many children appreciate patterns, as they often like things to be ordered, or in their right place. Making their own printed patterns can help them learn how to organize their ideas, and improve their coordination. Try to encourage them to work from left to right across the paper, as this will help them with their reading later.

Useful tip

You could add a little glitter to the paint for printing, to create some sparkly pictures or giftwrap.

Printed giftwrap

Print a simple two-color pattern from left to right, such as a row of red prints then a row of blue prints, and ask your child to copy it.

Draw a line and see if your child can make a series of prints just above it. Praise the outcome, however wonky, as they are mastering several skills at once.

Let your child cover a sheet of paper with printed patterns to make giftwrap. (Brown wrapping paper or rolled art project paper work well.)

Cutting and pasting

Children can use old magazines, catalogs and giftwrap for cutting and pasting. With some washable glue or a glue stick and a pair of scissors, most children will happily spend time choosing, cutting out and pasting pictures. These pages suggest some activities, but let children decide what they want to do, too.

Mastering scissors... and glue

For a young child, using a pair of scissors takes practice and you can help by holding the paper while they cut. Plastic scissors will cut paper, but ones with round-ended metal blades cut thicker things, so are a better buy. To start, children could just snip scraps of paper. In time, you could draw some large shapes for them to cut out. (Remove any excess paper that makes controlling the scissors even harder.) Younger children find ripping paper easier. They could use ripped strips to create their own pictures.

Let young children try tearing different kinds of paper, such as construction, tissue, or handmade paper.

Remember to dress children in plastic overalls or old clothes for cutting and pasting, and tie back long hair.

Useful tip

Left-handed scissors can make cutting easier for a left-handed child. Good toy stores sell or will order them for you.

The best glue for paper-sticking is a glue stick or white glue. Try a glue spatula and a brush, and see which you both prefer. You'll need to demonstrate how much glue to use and where to put it. Never let children use instant bonding glue or solvent glues that give off strong fumes.

Cut it out

Although it is very satisfying for a child to be let loose with an old magazine with a pair of scissors, here are some ways of taking the activity a little further and developing its interest for them.

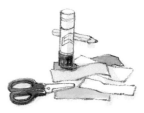

You can buy glue sticks and children's scissors in stationers and craft stores.

• Ask the child to look through the magazine for pictures of specific things, such as animals or trees. Suggest pasting them down to make a zoo or farm.

• Suggest children cut out some pictures of food and choose what they want to paste onto a paper plate to make their favorite meal.

• Try cutting some triangular flag shapes and taping these to some string. You can change the display regularly.

• Let your child choose pictures to decorate a cardboard toy box. Discuss how to paste them on – close together, spaced out or overlapping?

Safety point

Young children can choke on dried beans. Supervise very carefully if you provide them.

Making collages

Making a collage is really just pasting all kinds of things onto paper, which young children invariably enjoy. You could start a collection of things to paste down – old magazines, advertising handouts, pieces of colored paper and scraps of foil are all useful. On the right are some more ideas for things to use.

Strips of torn colored paper and simple shapes can be used to make a collage.

Leaves

Dried beans

Candy wrappers

Cotton balls

Feathers

Junk modeling

You may not see much potential in empty food boxes, plastic bottles and a roll of masking tape, but most young children enjoy making models out of junk. Finding out how to attach different things together, what works and what collapses, and seeing some of their ideas become 'real', gives children the chance to start understanding how simple technology works, too.

What do they need?

The main thing to remember is that everything children use for modeling must be clean, and safe. Germs grow quickly in dirty food containers, and anything with sharp or rough edges, or that has contained chemicals such as bleach, is not suitable. This still leaves a huge amount of throwaway packaging to be turned into models of rockets, castles or fireworks. You will also need tape and glue to stick things together. White glue adheres to things that are heavier and less absorbent than paper, and masking tape can be easier to handle and paint over than clear tape.

Cereal boxes, egg cartons and other packaging can all be used for junk models.

Children are rarely short of ideas for things to make from what you might have thrown away.

Try any of the following for junk modeling:

- Cardboard boxes
- Plastic food and yogurt cartons
- Bubble wrap
- Cardboard tubes
- Plastic milk or juice containers
- Egg cartons
- Plastic lids from jars
- Paper cups, plates and bowls
- Foil and plastic containers

Half a plastic bottle

Paper plate wheels

Simple models

It's a good idea to let children make whatever they want with the junk you have collected. This is how they discover what works, and what doesn't. Try not to look puzzled if their 'car' looks nothing like one; just ask them to tell you about it, and praise their work. There are some ideas for models on the Usborne Quicklinks Website (see page 120).

Young children will need help with the trickier cutting such as windows and doors, but leave the pasting and finer details to them.

Boxes, cups and tubes are easily taped together to make robots or funny monsters.

Hammer and nails

Many children are eager to do things they see grown-ups doing. Banging nails into pieces of wood to join them together may sound simple enough to adults, but many young children really enjoy making basic wooden models. If you supervise at all times, it's fine to let them nail or glue pieces of scrap wood together, screw in some screws, or use sandpaper to make rough edges smooth.

Child-size tool-kits make modeling with wood easier, as do longer nails that are not too thick, and soft wood.

Dough modeling

Most young children enjoy playing with modeling dough. They love tearing, snipping, thumping, rolling out, or just squeezing it – all of which are great fun, and excellent for their coordination skills. When they make dough models, they are using their imagination to create something different every time. They are also finding out what makes models look good, stay together… or fall apart.

You can buy several kinds of modeling dough; some are easier for small fingers to mold than others.

Useful tip

Cover the floor and tie back long hair before dough-play. If pieces get stuck in carpets, leave them to harden before vacuuming them out.

Modeling dough recipe

- 1 cup of all-purpose flour
- 1/2 cup salt
- 1 tablespoon vegetable oil
- 2 teaspoons cream of tartar
- 1 cup water
- A few drops of food coloring

1. Put the flour, salt, oil and cream of tartar into a large saucepan.

2. In a container, mix together the food coloring and water. Add the mixture to the saucepan and stir well.

3. Put the pan over a low heat and cook, stirring constantly until the dough becomes stiff.

4. Scrape the dough from the pan. When it's cool enough, knead until it is smooth.

Make your own dough

It's cheaper to make your own dough, using the recipe on the left, and it's not difficult. If you keep this dough in an airtight container or plastic bag in the refrigerator, it will keep well for several weeks. Try adding glitter, or a few drops of food coloring or peppermint essence to the dough. Make sure children don't eat any modeling dough, however. You could build up a collection of modeling tools from everyday objects, such as those below.

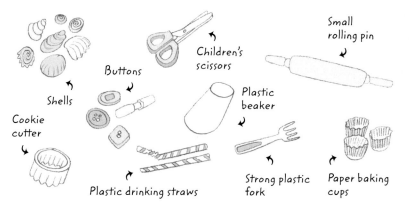

Shells

Cookie cutter

Buttons

Plastic drinking straws

Children's scissors

Plastic beaker

Strong plastic fork

Small rolling pin

Paper baking cups

Dough models

Although children will enjoy being able to do what they want with modeling dough, many like making something specific, too. Here are some models to suggest:

• Make a snail by winding a coil of dough into a shell and rolling a sausage shape for the body.

• Flatten a big lump of dough into a circle for a pizza, and make toppings from smaller pieces.

• Make a snake, a flower, a monster, a car, a dragon, a teddy bear (or anything else you can think of).

Put real candles on a model birthday cake and let your child enjoy blowing them out.

You can bake models made from homemade dough in a hot oven for about 20 minutes, until hard. When cool, children can paint and keep them. There are more dough-play ideas on the Usborne Quicklinks Website (see page 120).

Models to eat

Model-making with some bread dough, or some ready-roll pastry, is fun. It can be a useful activity for children to do while you cook, and it gives them an edible result. They could learn how to make a dough twist, or some pastry people. Some children may want to make more elaborate models, such as animals or cars.

Make sure children wash their hands well before making edible models.

Useful tip

It's probably not a good idea to let very young children play with potter's clay. It is hard for little hands to mold and it can be messy and stain things.

Make a face from a flat circle and some thin rolls of dough or pastry.

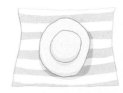

Make a mini-loaf from two balls of dough of different sizes.

Papier-mâché models

Papier-mâché models are made from strips of paper dipped into glue, stuck on in layers and left to harden completely. It may take a day or more for them to do so. It can be a messy process, but as long as the table is covered with a wipeable cloth before you begin, mess should be easy to deal with.

Useful tip

You can mix your own paste for papier-mâché using flour and water. Mix one part flour to two parts water.

For papier-mâché, you'll need glue or paste and plenty of old newspaper to tear into strips.

Balloon ↲

Make a piñata for parties from a balloon shape — fill it with candy, seal it, hang it up and take turns hitting it with a stick.

Make a brightly colored fish with cardboard fins and long, tissue-paper streamers for a tail.

Make a big pig by sticking on parts of an egg box for legs and the bottom part of a paper cup for a nose.

It's easiest to start papier-mâché by building around a mold, such as a blown-up balloon, following the steps below. Once the balloon shape is dry, it can be adapted and painted to make any of the ideas on the left.

1. Put some paper glue in a bowl or mix flour and water. Tear paper into strips 1 1/2 x 2 inches. Blow up a balloon and knot it.

2. Holding the balloon steady, let children dip each strip in glue, then press it on the balloon. Overlap the strips, adding lots of layers.

3. Let the shape dry, then use a pin to pop the balloon. Paint the shape with ready-mixed or powder paint.

Music and songs

Most young children like singing, dancing, or banging on a drum, and giving them the opportunity to enjoy all kinds of music, whenever you can, has many other benefits. It can help them learn to listen, build their self-confidence, give them the chance to explore and express their feelings and even develop math skills. Some more benefits of musical play are listed below.

Sing and dance

Listening to music helps children interpret things they hear and can help with other areas of learning.

Singing helps children learn how to control, and use their voices effectively.

Making music is fun for children by themselves, with you, or with other children.

Learning the words of songs and rhymes helps children expand their vocabulary.

Dancing to music is good exercise, and helps children's physical coordination.

Listen and learn

For many people, music plays an important part in everyday life. It can make us feel relaxed, cheer us up, give us energy – or make us feel sad. Young children can experience music in much the same way as adults do – all they need are lots of chances to develop their listening skills. Here are some ways to encourage them.

Classical music often fascinates young children...

...but they may also enjoy the beat of a military march...

...some jazz...

...or a thudding bassline.

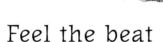

Listening is a skill that needs to be developed, so listen to music together as often as you can.

Feel the beat

Understanding and managing their emotions is one of the hardest skills children need to learn, and music can give them the chance to explore feelings and moods. This activity encourages them to think and talk about their feelings. You need to choose a varied selection of music before you begin.

Useful tip

Playing fast, lively music can help give tired 'whining' children some energy, just as slow, soothing music can calm them down.

1. Tell your child you are going to play some pieces of music and you want to know what they think about them.

2. As you play each piece, your child can just listen or move around to the music. Does their face tell you anything?

3. Talk about each piece afterwards. What did it make them want to do, or feel? Did it make you feel the same?

Musical games

Research shows that musical games can really help children learn to listen. The skills they need to play these games include concentrating, recognizing patterns, following instructions and remembering things in order – all useful in other areas of learning, such as math. Here are some games to try:

• Party games, such as musical statues and musical chairs, help children learn to listen carefully for when the music starts and stops.

• Encourage children to copy you when you sing quickly, slowly, loudly, softly or at a high pitch. This develops their musical awareness.

• Clap out a simple beat and see if your child can clap with you, then alone. Can your child clap a beat for you to copy?

In a game of musical statues children must freeze when the music stops.

Let's sing

Many adults only dare to sing when they think no one can hear them, but young children feel no such embarrassment, so you don't need to feel shy about singing with them. Remember that nobody is judging you after all. Singing just because it makes you feel good is one of the biggest benefits music can bring, and one that's really worth sharing with children. Singing songs and nursery rhymes is important for children's language development too (see page 32).

Useful tip
Pitch songs fairly low when singing with children and try simple, short songs with repetition or counting. There are some ideas on page 32.

Making music

Many young children like listening to music, but most enjoy making it even more. Their music-making may involve some degree of patience on your part as the sounds they produce may not, at first, be your idea of tuneful. Remember, however, that making music can give children an enormous sense of pride and satisfaction, and though most will be too young for music lessons yet, research shows that letting them make music is beneficial in many ways. So try to forget grown-up expectations of what sounds good… or doesn't, and let them have fun.

Make your own instruments

There are, of course, lots of toy musical instruments you can buy, but many homemade versions can be just as satisfying and provide plenty of musical entertainment. On the left are three very simple instruments that you could make together. Young children will also enjoy playing smaller 'real' instruments, such as bells, triangles, tambourines and castanets.

Rubber bands

Stretch four rubber bands of different thicknesses tightly over an old tissue box (or cut a hole in a small cardboard box). Let children strum the bands.

Metal spoon

Pour different amounts of water into glass bottles and let children tap them gently with a spoon. Each note of this 'xylophone' sounds different.

To make maracas (shakers), put some dried beans or plastic beads into clean plastic bottles. Screw the lids on firmly and seal with tape.

Learning to listen, and to take turns, are important skills.

Recording stars

Recording children's music-making gives them a chance to listen to it again and talk about what they hear. You could try recording some outdoor and indoor sounds for them to recognize, too. On the right are some more suggestions for making recordings together.

Taking turns can be difficult for young children. Making music with others (and recording the results) can help them learn that, if everyone plays at once, it doesn't sound as good – but if they take turns, it sounds better. Try letting your child play or sing one verse of a song, and you, or their friend, the next.

Castanets

Tambourine

Playing simple instruments such as tambourines, castanets, shakers, bells and triangles can give children a lot of enjoyment.

Things to record

• Encourage a child to experiment by making lots of different sounds. Can they roar, hum, buzz, hiss and whisper?

• Record yourselves singing some songs or rhymes. Your child may want to add an instrumental accompaniment.

• If you hum a simple tune, can they make up some words? Complete nonsense is fine! When everyone's ready, record the new song.

• Record a child making some sound effects to accompany you telling a story. (If they get too loud, remind them they won't hear the words.)

Sssshh...

For some young children, their only volume level seems to be maximum. If this sounds familiar, try some games with a 'whispering tube'. Find a long carboard tube and explain to children that they can only whisper to you, or each other, down the tube, otherwise the game won't work, or they'll hurt everyone's ears. Over time, this self-control should help turn the volume down.

Useful tip

Let children hear live music if you can. Stop if someone is playing music nearby, or find out if there are any children's concerts you could go to.

Songs and rhymes

Young children usually enjoy singing songs and rhymes, and these are an excellent way of developing musical awareness. Singing songs also helps children develop an appreciation for rhyme and rhythm and an awareness of how words sound, both of which are essential pre-reading skills. Many nursery rhymes and songs also introduce important concepts such as counting, time, and weather.

Action rhymes, clapping songs and fingerplay rhymes all involve doing movements to the words, and learning how and when to do these actions develops children's memory skills as well as their physical coordination. On the left are two good ones to try. You can hear their tunes, and several others, on the Usborne Quicklinks Website (see page 120).

Performing actions gets children moving and helps their coordination.

Row, Row, Row your Boat

(Sit on floor, facing partner, hold hands and row.)

Row, row, row your boat,
Gently down the stream;
Merrily, merrily,
Merrily, merrily,
Life is but a dream.

Row, row, row your boat,
Gently down the stream;
If you see a crocodile,
Don't forget to SCREAM!

(Jump up and scream if you see a crocodile!)

The Wheels on the Bus

(Spin forearms around each other to make the wheels.)

The wheels on the bus go
round and round,
round and round,
round and round;
The wheels on the bus go
round and round, all day long.

Verses include:
Doors go open and shut/
Wipers go swish, swish, swish/
Horn goes beep, beep, beep/
Babies go 'wah, wah, wah'...

Make-believe

For young children, and those caring for them, pretend play is very much a part of daily life. After their third birthday, most children start to invent more elaborate make-believe games than just dressing-up, which they may have enjoyed when they were toddlers. By this stage, they start really trying to imagine what it might be like to be someone else. This part of a young child's development is called role-playing, and it's a good idea to encourage it for many reasons.

Who shall I be?

Children benefit from playing with others in make-believe games; working out characters and settings develops their social skills.

By acting out situations they have seen, even sad ones, children often begin to feel they understand them better.

In games, children can be the parent, the person in charge, as they can't in real life. It's good for them to try out being the boss.

Make-believe can be exciting. Children can zoom into space, cross raging rivers, fly through the air or put fires out!

Being other people, solving problems and working together helps young children learn, quite simply, how to think.

Let's pretend

As you watch young children play, you may often see them pretending to be someone else, somewhere else, and they may well have different voices, movements and behavior to match. Some children even have a pretend friend who they talk to and play with. Although it's generally a good idea to encourage pretend play, there are some aspects of it that experts disagree about, so parents and caregivers can be left confused as to how to avoid any problems. On these pages are some guidelines to help you.

Firstly, you don't have to spend a lot to encourage pretend play. Most children are happy to invent games with basic accessories, such as hats and scarves. Some do pester for 'real' costumes, and you need to decide if they will play with them enough to justify the cost.

Research shows that some children feel more secure with costumes or props in their pretend games.

Older children often enjoy pretend play more with their friends.

About war games

• Many children (especially boys) invent games that involve fighting or battles, or ask for 'realistic' war toys, but most preschools and day cares ban toy weapons, as some childcare professionals believe that these can make children aggressive.

• Other experts say there's no evidence of any long-lasting harm, and that war games are natural. They think that forbidding such games may just make them seem more attractive to some young children.

War toys

Perhaps the main problem for caregivers in pretend play surrounds war games and toys, such as guns and swords. There's been a lot of research in this area, but experts still disagree about whether or not children should be allowed to play with these toys (see left). If you don't want to buy war toys, that's fine. Whatever you decide, try, above all, to help children understand that hurting people is wrong.

Show me how you feel

One of the main benefits for children in pretending to be someone else is that they can express feelings that they can't do as themselves. If they are pretending to be 'the bossy lady in the library', they may behave with pretty convincing bossiness. Sometimes, however, make-believe games may be less comfortable for you to hear. Children may treat toys unkindly, or always take the lead in games, telling other children what to do. If you can, try not to interfere unless things get out of hand. This is how young children find out about feelings – theirs and other people's.

• If a child wants to be a parent for a while, you could play along and be the child. Most young children enjoy this role-reversal.

• Some preschools won't mind if a child wants to come dressed as Batman (but check first). Being a superhero for a day may even help a child's self-confidence.

Dressing up

Dressing up is an important part of play that helps children understand more about people and the world. Children sometimes act out the roles of people they see around them and favorite characters in books. Whatever or whoever they choose to be, it's important to encourage this type of play, as research suggests that it improves children's language and literacy, and also helps their emotional development.

These girls are enjoying dressing up as princesses.

Cardboard boxes and tubes are ideal for making masks, knights' shields or astronauts' helmets.

Safety point

Children shouldn't play with clothes with long cords or sashes that could get tangled. Adult-sized, or high-heeled, shoes are not safe, either as children may trip while trying to walk in them.

Who am I?

Toddlers often imitate things they see people doing, but by the time children are about three years old, their ability to pretend to be someone else is much greater. You may find them absorbed in being an astronaut, princess or police officer, and see them inventing elaborate games for their imaginary character. This page has lots of ideas for encouraging this role-play.

Providing props

For many roles, jewelry and bags from a consignment or thrift store work well, as will different pieces of fabric for children to make into cloaks or saris. Childcare workers often find that children will play more imaginary games if they are given time to adapt the things around them, making a sofa into a ship or the space under a table into a cave.

Sometimes, however, children's games can be richer if more specific props are available. A magic wand and some wings will be appreciated by a child who wants to be a fairy. A toy hairbrush and hairdryer may make a game of hairstylist much more satisfying, too.

Dolls and a toy doctor's kit provide plenty of scope for make-believe games.

Who shall I be?

Most young children need very little encouragement to begin role-play. Looking at storybooks together, or books about people and what jobs they do, can be good starting points for those who need help with ideas. There are some more suggestions on the right.

A teddy bear might become a real wild bear in a role-play.

• Build up a collection of hats, crowns and helmets. This helps children be firefighters, police officers, chefs, queens or cowboys/girls.

• A lot of children's fun with dressing up comes from seeing themselves in their finery. Take photos or let them parade in front of a mirror.

• Offer children variety in who they role-play with — sometimes with other children, sometimes on their own, or with you.

The same game

Sometimes, young children can get stuck in a rut, only ever acting out the roles of characters on television or in cartoons, for example. This is quite normal, but some experts, parents and caregivers worry in case this limits a child's imagination. If it bothers you, try suggesting something new, such as 'Maybe we could set up a hospital over here', or find a new prop to use – such as a magic key. Many children respond well to having the scene set in this way. Below are some easy ways of encouraging children to explore some everyday situations in role-play.

It really doesn't matter if a police officer wants to work on a building site.

• Set out some toys in rows along the floor as if in hospital beds. Ask the children what illness each one has, and how they'll make them all better.

• A toy phone, pencil and paper on a table are a fine make-believe office. If children can use a computer, or just tap on a keyboard, even better.

• A selection of toy plates, silverware, pans, a table and chair could be any type of restaurant. Customers could eat with chopsticks or fingers, too.

• A toy cash register and money, plus a variety of objects can stock a store. Ask the 'storeowner' how much things cost, and let your child help you count the money.

Shows and stories

Most games that involve make-believe don't need any planning, but happen naturally as children play together. Others, such as the ideas on these pages, need a little more organization, so children may need your help with them.

Changing faces

Painting a child's face immediately transforms their image of themselves. However simple the design, most children are thrilled to see themselves as a tiger, superhero or dog. Before you use face paints for the first time, make sure children are not allergic to them by painting a small patch on their skin and leaving it for several hours. When you are ready to start, make sure your hands and the child's face are clean and dry and follow the guidelines on the left.

Useful tip

Young children will probably really enjoy painting your face. Let them have a try. It washes off, after all.

Face painting

• Use water-based face paints, as they go on well with a sponge and wash off fairly easily.

• Make sure that children are wearing old clothes or a plastic apron before you start. Tie back long hair.

• It's a good idea to sponge on a paint base in one color first. Then, use a fine brush for details.

There are some face-painting designs to try on the Usborne Quicklinks Website.

Some simple masks to make from cardboard:

Teddy bear ↘

Clown ↖

Super-hero ↗

Masks also help children get into character. There are lots available to buy, but you can make your own from basic materials. You could cut a mask shape from cardboard and let children adapt it – there's an easy first pattern and more ideas, on the Usborne Quicklinks Website (see page 120).

Storytellers

Starting at about three years old, many children are eager to act out favorite stories. You may notice them saying a story, or part of it, aloud as they play, or adapting a story in their own way. You could suggest children act out a story they know well as you narrate it. If this is too hard, they could add sound effects, such as the wolf's knock at the little pigs' door. Many fairytales are ideal for this type of play, but younger children may not cope with complicated ones.

Some simple accessories and props can help a child become Little Red Riding Hood, the big, bad wolf or Grandmother.

Putting on a show

Many preschools and kindergartens put on shows, giving parents and caregivers the opportunity to see their children sing songs, or act out a simple story. There's no need for you to stage such elaborate productions at home, but many children are eager to put on shows. On the right are some tips to make the experience positive for all of you.

Plays and shows

• Organizing a show is a good way for children to learn how to plan and cooperate with each other, so if you can, leave them to it.

• Young children often try to do something too tricky and need help to keep things simple, so be on hand to give help if they ask for it.

• When the show is about to begin, leave the chores, put your chair in front of the stage area and give the performers your full attention.

• Give them lots of applause, even if the play made no sense to you. They will have learned a lot while making it up and performing it for you.

The benefits of puppets

• Puppets help children express their feelings, through what they make a puppet say, or do.

• It can be easier for children to talk about how a puppet feels than how a person might.

• Shy children often feel more confident when talking to or acting as a puppet's character.

Small box

Small paper bags or boxes make simple puppets. Children can draw or stick on features.

Wooden spoon

A wooden spoon can be decorated with a face and stuck-on hair and clothes.

Paper eyes

Old sock

An old sock can be made into a puppet. You need to pull in the toe to form a mouth.

Puppet play

Children have played with puppets for thousands of years, and puppet shows are still used to tell stories in many parts of the world. Their appeal to children is so great that many popular characters on children's television are puppets. Whether they are simply played with like dolls, or in a show, puppets can bring children a lot of pleasure. Childcare professionals have also found that playing with puppets is really valuable for young children in the ways described on the left.

Simple glove puppets are ideal for small hands. Children can play two characters at once by putting one on each hand.

Making puppets

Try giving children the chance to be really creative with puppets by letting them make their own – it's not difficult. This way, they can think and talk about the puppet's character as they design what it looks like. They can make puppets from paper or cardboard, either to fit over their whole hands, or just over each finger. On the left are three easy ones to try.

Puppet shows

Puppet shows are a good, clear way of getting a story or message across to young children. Often, children who have enjoyed seeing a puppet show want to put on their own, but may need your help to make it work. It's tricky for them to get the right puppet to say the right thing at the right time, on stage, so keep things relaxed.

If several children are doing a show, they will need to discover how to cooperate for it to work. What they will gain from the experience is, hopefully, worth all your patience and their hard work. Most children will just be happy to crouch behind a sofa, using the back of it as their puppets' stage.

Find out how to make these pirate finger puppets on the Usborne Quicklinks Website (see page 120).

Children often find even a simple puppet show engrossing.

Useful tip
A few children are alarmed by the way some puppets move or sound. Bear this in mind before booking a puppet show for a party.

Shadow puppets

Shadow puppets are shapes that cast a shadow against a wall or through a screen. Children may enjoy cutting out different shapes from cardboard and taping a stick to them. Shine a lamp at the shapes so children can see the shadows dance on the wall when they move the puppets, but make sure no one touches the hot lamp or lightbulb.

Bird shapes with big beaks and long tails make good shadow puppets.

Mini-worlds

When young children play with miniature toys, such as cars, animals or dolls, they are inventing their own, smaller versions of the world they see around them. Childcare professionals call this 'small world play'. Some of its many benefits are outlined on the left.

This is my world

Experts have found that the way young children enjoy small world play changes during their preschool years. Starting at around three years old, most children start to arrange their toy cars, dolls or houses carefully, often talking to themselves as they play, and treating each toy as an individual. They know who lives in which house, drives which car, or sits in which chair.

To them, these mini-worlds seem very real, and some children get so involved in small world play that they can seem a little obsessed with their games, and with the toys involved. Don't worry if this is the case in your home – it's natural. This is one of the few areas of their lives that young children can control, so it's important to let them do so if you can.

Benefits of small world play

• As children create a small world, they make decisions about how things should be organized, all the time.

• Moving small toys around helps improve children's coordination, and what are known as fine motor skills.

• Being the 'boss' in games allows children to act out situations from the big world, and understand these better.

• Small world play gives children the chance to sort their toys into colors, types, or families — which is a basic first math skill.

When children are involved in small world play, encourage them to talk about the world they are creating to improve their language skills.

Setting it up

There are some small world 'settings' that remain popular, however much toy fashions change. If you aren't sure which a child might enjoy, here are some favorites to choose from:

- towns, with houses and roads
- farms and farmyards
- pet stores and zoos
- dolls and doll's houses
- train and car sets
- building sites

Useful tip
Some children like to collect small toys. You could buy one to add to their collection when they deserve a treat, or to encourage good behavior.

Toy stores sell a huge range of all of these types of toys, but an elaborate doll's house is not necessarily any more exciting to play with than a selection of little houses or plastic figures. Often, a basic model town, a family of dolls or a few little animals provide a child with more play opportunities than a ready-made fantasy doll house. Also, as children inevitably grow out of these kinds of toys you can often pick them up second-hand.

Let children decide where things go in their mini-world, even if the arrangement looks chaotic to you.

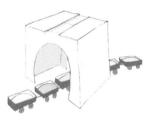

Use a craft knife and some paint to transform cardboard boxes into tunnels, train sheds or the rooms of a house.

You could draw roads, traffic lights and traffic circles onto a big sheet of paper or cardboard for toy cars to go on trips.

On the right are some ideas for making simple settings or landscapes for small worlds. To make something a little more permanent, you could stick some green fabric and a foil pond onto a sheet of thick cardboard to make a farm, or draw a layout of railroad track for trains. The whole thing can be put safely away after play.

Some toy animals could set off on a desert trek in the sandpit, or a big bowl of water become a busy harbor full of boats.

Dens and playhouses

You may not remember much about your own early childhood, but the chances are that you will remember building dens, or finding hidey holes, to play in. A visit to a playgroup or day care can give children the chance to play in sophisticated toy playhouses, but at home, you can help them experience the same play opportunities with much simpler materials, using the ideas on the left.

Many children want to make real little homes inside their dens, taking in cushions to make somewhere to sleep, food to eat and toys to play with. They may need help to build play spaces like this, but a lot of their enjoyment is in organizing them just the way they want them.

Don't come in!

Young children have very few opportunities to lay down the rules, but inside their dens, they're the boss. It's good to give them the chance to play in private from time to time. If they invite you in, that's fine; if they tell you to keep out, try not to feel hurt. Respecting their wishes in such small things can help build trust in your relationship.

Drape a blanket over a table top, or over a clothes-drying rack to make a hidden space for children to play in.

A very large cardboard box with both ends opened out makes a good tunnel to crawl through, or hide in.

Outside, a sheet or blanket hung over a clothesline or rope and weighted or pegged at the corners makes a basic tent.

Some garden canes tied at one end and covered with a blanket makes a tepee. Tape over any sharp cane-ends.

Books and stories

It's really important to encourage children to learn to love books. Reading with them helps them learn everyday skills, such as how to speak, listen and understand language, as well as developing pre-reading skills. It will also help them to use their imagination. Whether they prefer fairy tales, tales about trains, or hearing how tractors work, try to make time each day to read books with young children.

What's so good about books?

Children who enjoy books from their early years are far more likely to become good, avid readers.

Looking at books teaches skills, such as how to turn pages, notice details and follow a storyline.

Children may meet new words, ideas or situations in a book. Through them, they can begin to learn to think.

Books can help satisfy children's curiosity, answer their questions and build their general knowledge.

Reading with a young child helps them understand that the black shapes on the page (letters and words) can be decoded and have meaning.

Good books

There are very few playthings that can give children as much pleasure as the time they spend reading a story, or sharing a good book with you. Studies show that it's important for their future reading skills for children to get used to looking at books as often as possible and 'book time' should be especially enjoyable for them because they have your undivided attention. These pages give you some simple ideas for making books part of your daily life. If you're not sure about how to go about finding books that your child might enjoy, the hints on the left may help.

Books on a subject a child is interested in are often a good starting point.

If there's no rush, it's fine to read the same story six times...

Which books?

• Ask friends with children which books they recommend. They might be willing to lend you some so you can see if your child enjoys them too.

• Trying borrowing a few books at a time from a library. Let children choose the ones they want, or ask librarians for help, if they get stuck.

• Don't be afraid to ask for help in bookstores. Booksellers know a lot about what kinds of books suit different children.

Time for books

You need to build book time into each day with young children, but it will only work when they are not very tired, restless or hungry. If you are too busy, explain this and ask them to wait. Many people share stories after a meal, or at bedtime, as a regular, quieter, treat. Book time is a good way of making you sit down for a while – and if you look forward to it, so will your child. Turn the television off, forget the housework and enjoy this together-time.

Books at home

Letting children see you reading books, magazines, catalogs and newspapers helps show them that you think reading is important and enjoyable. Make sure boys see their dads reading as often as possible, so they don't get the idea that reading is only for girls. Here are more ways of getting the best out of books with young children:

• Let children linger over pictures in books if they want to. For them, they are often as important as hearing the words.

• Involve children whenever you can. Encourage them to turn pages, spot things in pictures, or act out the stories.

• Talk about the book together. What will happen next? Do they like the story? But keep it relaxed — it's not a test!

When you are looking at books together, snuggle up somewhere cozy to make book time special.

Tell me a story

Looking at familiar books is often reassuring for children. The fact that they are always the same is comforting if a child is unwell, or has had a change in routine, for instance. Try recording yourself reading some favorite stories aloud, and playing them to a child. You can take story tapes or CDs on long car rides, too, to fend off boredom. For many people, the books they enjoyed when they were little become treasured childhood memories. Those are just what you're aiming to create when you share books with children.

Keep a box of books in the room young children play in, so that they can dip into it whenever they want to.

Books and beyond

Books are useful for more than just the stories, pictures or information they contain; they are rich sources of ideas for other activities, too, as you'll see from the ideas shown on these pages. Younger children may need more help with some of the activities, and older ones may want to take them a little further. Whatever they do, the key is to let them enjoy it and see books as fun.

Finding out more

It can sometimes seem as if young children ask questions all day, and there are bound to be some you can't answer, or feel you don't know enough about to answer correctly. These are ideal times to show them that books can answer such questions, and provide information. You could take the general approach described on the left.

Some children develop a particular interest in something, such as machines or animals. Buying or borrowing some books about these things encourages their curiosity. Such simple actions mean a lot to children: you have recognized and encouraged their interest, and given them the possibility of finding out more.

Why? What? How?

• If a child asks: 'Where does my food go?', for example, answer them in a couple of sentences, in simple language.

• When you next visit a library or bookstore, look for children's books with clear diagrams of inside the body.

• Show the child the diagrams, pointing out things they will know such as the mouth, throat, stomach and bottom.

• Let them see that you look things up in books, too, if you don't know something or want to find out more.

If a child wants to know more about a pet, books can provide the answer.

Books can help encourage a child's particular interest.

What's in a story?

Stories can lead to many imaginary games as children pretend to be the characters and relive the tale. Stories can also help children understand that things often happen in a certain order, or sequence. Realizing that stories have a beginning, a middle and an end is a milestone – and some experts think that when you read to young children it's important always to read to the end of a story, to make this point clear. Games based on stories that ask a child to put things in order are usually popular.

• Choose a favorite story and talk about what happens in it with your child. Try leaving gaps in the story and letting them fill them in.

• Let children draw pictures showing what happens in a favorite story. If you mix up the order, can they put them right again?

Children often enjoy acting out a sequence from a story – crawling under the fence, through the long grass and between the tall trees...

Start with a story

Making up stories may seem hard at first, but children usually really enjoy them. Use a picture, object or photo for inspiration, or something the child has done. Young children often request more of a made-up story that has really captured their imagination. If you can, build a cliffhanger into the ending each time, so that one of you can take the story further the next time.

Talking about stories, and which ones you both like best, is good. Try putting a selection of storybooks into a bag and letting a child dip in and choose one for you both to read together. Did your child like the story?

An object such as a hat, a pair of glasses or a necklace can be a good starting point for making up a story.

Make a book

1. To make a book about your child, help them choose some photos of themselves as a baby and toddler.

2. Stick the photos into a scrapbook in time order. Add some of their drawings, or souvenirs from trips.

3. Write a sentence or two on each page, telling the 'story' of the child's life. They may want to tell you what to put.

4. Keep adding to the book. Over time, children may want to do all the writing. The book will grow with them.

Useful tip

Next time a child deserves a treat, let them choose a children's comic, magazine or book, rather than a toy or candy.

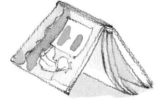

More to do with books

Most young children enjoy stories, but there are some who don't find it easy to sit still and listen, so getting them to love books can be more of a struggle. Some experts argue that modern life is so fast, it's more important than ever to let children experience quieter, more thoughtful activities, such as sharing books with you.

Try to make sure dads, granddads or big brothers read and share books with little boys. Research shows that boys in particular can take longer to start to enjoy books. It doesn't matter if all they ever want are books about football or bulldozers – it's looking at books that counts.

A book about me

There are few subjects young children find more interesting than themselves, so making a book of pictures and text with your child as its 'star' may work well for a child who is more reluctant to look at books. On the left are some hints on how to go about this.

Don't worry too much about how young children choose to 'read' their books, but make sure they learn not to damage them.

Letters
and numbers

Letters and numbers are all around us, every
day, and most young children are aware of them
long before they start school. The ideas in this part of
the book suggest some ways of preparing children for the
reading, writing and math they will learn when they
go to preschool or kindergarten. The activities are simple
and enjoyable and aim, above all, to help children
understand how letters and numbers work.

a, b, c... 1, 2, 3

Pointing out letters and numbers in daily life helps children
become familiar with them, and what they mean.

Playing letter and number games helps children see them
as fun, rather than something tricky to be learned.

Young children love the chance to count, measure, spot,
write — and generally just show you how much they know.

Reading, writing and using numbers are all essential skills,
so it's good to give children a confident start in all three.

See if a child can figure out what sound the animal in a picture begins with.

Rhyming games

• Try leaving out the rhyming word in a nursery rhyme or rhyming story, and see if the child can figure out what it could be.

• Try making a deliberate mistake and see if the child notices. Say 'fish' instead of 'dish' for instance. The sillier, the better.

Useful tip

For young children, a letter is just another shape. They need to see it many times before they remember what it means.

Letter games

Many people who care for young children feel anxious about the best way of introducing them to letters and reading. Experts believe that the best thing you can do is play games and do enjoyable activities that involve letters. This way, children will learn in a fun, relaxed way.

Preschools and kindergartens help children learn letter sounds before they look at letter shapes. Making the link between the two is the basis of learning to read; writing letters usually comes later. You can help young children learn these skills at home as they play, as part of everyday life. There are more ideas for letter-learning activities and games that involve letters on the Usborne Quicklinks Website (see page 120).

Rhyming games

Reading rhyming stories and playing rhyming games can really help children develop an awareness of the different, and similar, sounds in words they hear. If your child doesn't understand 'rhymes with', say 'sounds like' instead, but most children soon understand what rhymes are and enjoy recognizing them. On the left are two easy games to try.

Once they've gotten the hang of it, children may enjoy playing rhyming games together.

Everyday letters

The more children see letters in their everyday lives, the easier they will find it to recognize them. Look for the letter that starts their name, or another letter they already know in as many places as possible. Here are some more ways to introduce letters:

• Look at alphabet books together. Stick to capitals, not small letters at first, as these are the ones children will learn first at school. Point to and sound out each letter together.

• Go on a letter hunt from time to time. Look for letters on buses, signposts or packaging. Buy some lower-case letter magnets and let children enjoy playing with them.

• Cut out pictures of things that start with the same letter (or, first of all, the same sound – 'mmm' for example), and make your own alphabet frieze or scrapbook.

Look at letters in favorite books and alphabet books. Can children find any that they recognize?

Easy letter games

The activities below are easy to set up and can be done again and again. You need to make some letter cards, one for each letter of the alphabet. You can find out how to help children learn to form the letters (and make their sounds) on the Usborne Quicklinks Website (see page 120). You could laminate the cardboard before cutting it into squares, to make the cards last longer.

(see page 120)

Useful tip

Letter magnets help children see letters as something they can move around, and play with. They also help them begin to recognize letter shapes.

To make letter cards, draw lines on thin cardboard to make squares about 2 x 2 inches. Write the small letters of the alphabet on them and cut out.

Spot the letter – put all the cards in a bag. Let your child choose one and see if they know the sound. If not, they can put it back and choose another.

Mailing letters – cut a slot in a box and ask the child to mail a 'b' card to 'bear', for instance. Give them help with the letter sounds and shapes if they need it.

Three letter words – children may enjoy sounding out letters to make up easy, three-letter words such as 'cat' or 'dog'. Give them clues if necessary.

Give children a selection of pens, pencils and crayons to try 'writing' with.

Letter formation activities

• Finger-painting letter shapes can be easier than trying to write them. Children can make letters bigger, and clearer, too.

• Pour a thin layer of flour into a shallow tray and let children make letter shapes in it with their fingers.

• Let children write letter shapes with a brush covered with glue or a glue stick, then sprinkle on some glitter.

• Fill a clean, empty, squirt bottle with water and let children squirt letter shapes onto the ground outdoors.

• In the bathtub, draw some letters in the bubbles for your child to copy. Can you guess the letters they draw for you?

Let me write

Most children start to make marks on paper as toddlers, and between the ages of three and four they are very eager to do some 'real writing'. This page has some ideas for encouraging children's interest in writing, a skill that takes longer for them to master than recognizing letter sounds and shapes. The goal is to give them confidence, which will, in turn, help them when they start school.

First writing

You will probably find that children start to try to write without any help. It may not look like writing to you, but remember to encourage their efforts and don't correct them at this stage. To them, these squiggles have meaning and are their first writing and they'll be very proud of it.

Some children prefer being given writing to trace. Try writing some clear, capital letters in pale colored pencil or marker and letting your child trace over the top. Many children will be able to trace letters such as l, i, x, and v quite well by around four, and once able to do this for most letters, they can move on to copying letters you have written. On the left are more ways to encourage letter formation, without a pencil or paper.

Remember to praise all of a child's efforts at making letter shapes.

Learning about letters

Many young children develop a fascination with writing and letters, and are eager to know exactly what you are writing, why, and just how you are doing it. Let them see you writing by hand, and on a keyboard, whenever you can, so that they see that writing is important to you, too. There are many simple ways that you can encourage or extend their interest in learning about letters. On the right are some activities you could try together.

Children could draw the items you need for a shopping list and you could add the words.

Writing activities

• Let your child dictate a story to you as you write it down, or type it onto a computer. Then, you can read the story back to them.

• Can your child copy giant letters you chalk onto the ground or make in sand? Let children enjoy the freedom of writing on this scale as long as it isn't permanent.

• Tell your child what you're planning for a meal. Can they tell you some of the things you need to write on a shopping list of ingredients?

That's my name

Often, one of the first words young children recognize is their name. It may be one of the first words they write that you can recognize, too. These three easy activities give children opportunities to practice forming the letters of their names in everyday situations.

Useful tip

Some young children just aren't interested in writing yet. Keep encouraging them, let them see you writing, and don't worry about it.

Get children to make their name out of dough using letter-shaped cookie cutters or by shaping letters from rolled dough shapes.

Let a child tell you what to write on a postcard to Granny, or someone else they know. Let them sign it and add some kisses.

Suggest children write their names on labels and stick them onto their things. They'll soon learn that those letters mean them.

Sorting is a basic math skill: can children sort their toys into groups – people, vehicles and animals, for example?

Matching is the key to children's understanding of what makes things different from each other.

Matching also helps children understand what makes things alike in some way.

Mini-mathematicians

Young children learn math without even realizing it. Preschools, kindergartens and learning centers use all kinds of activities to help children understand how to put things in order, how to remember things, how to organize things into groups and finish patterns – all basic mathematical skills. The ideas here help to encourage children's confidence in thinking mathematically. You may need to adapt the activities to suit the age of your child.

Find it, sort it, match it

Being able to say where things are sounds simple, but in fact children need what are called positional words to be able to master this first math skill. These are words such as 'under', 'on top of' and 'in front of'. Children usually grasp these ideas quickly and learn them from using them in daily life, by saying 'it's under the chair' or 'behind the cushion'. Try to make sure you use positional words often.

Play 'Where's Teddy?' to help children practice positional words.

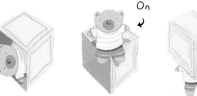

Most young children enjoy sorting things out – a skill experts call classifying. Many spend ages organizing their toys into colors, types or families. The activities below help children begin to make decisions about what belongs where… and why.

• Put all the family's shoes in a big pile on the floor and ask your child to sort them into pairs. Put the timer on for added excitement.

• Ask children if they can help you sort the laundry, and find all their own clothes, all the socks, or all the blue things for example.

• Give children some plastic bowls and colored counters or a selection of different pasta shapes to sort into colors or types.

Shape-spotting

The world is full of different shapes, and it is easier than you might think to help children recognize them. Cut sandwiches into triangles or squares and point their shape out to children. Ask your child what shape the television screen is or whether they'd like a round or a square cookie. Naming everyday shapes may feel a bit strange to you, but it's really valuable for a young child.

Set a challenge — can your child spot the triangular cookie on the plate?

Which comes next?

Recognizing, making and completing patterns involves children doing what is called sequencing – another early math skill. They usually make patterns naturally – in the way they line up toy cars, build with colored blocks or carefully arrange unwanted peas on their plate. It's a good idea to provide plenty of opportunities to play with patterns, as it helps develop logical thinking, learning to remember things and predicting what might come next.

Useful tip
You could adapt the pattern-making ideas below so they can be used with stickers. Colored stickers are available at most supermarkets.

1. Try arranging some colored blocks into a pattern and see if your child can continue it. Keep it simple: red, blue, red, blue...

2. If things go well, see if children are able to manage a trickier one such as blue, red, green, blue, red, green, blue...

3. Once they've mastered these simple patterns, you could try something harder still: red, blue, red, yellow, red, blue, red, yellow...

Everyday numbers

Young children learn to recognize and use numbers, and how to count in the same way as they learn anything else – through play and repetition. If you play number games with them, and encourage them to use and recognize numbers whenever you can, they will probably learn numbers easily. It helps if you touch, move or point to the things you are counting.

Most people who take care of young children find themselves counting stairs or spoonfuls of food without thinking about it. Every time you use numbers, it helps children remember them, but they may not yet understand that the word three, for example, means three things. To help them make this link, try the activities on the left.

These are some ways for children to practice counting in everyday situations:

• Put some grapes or cherries on a plate. Tell your child they can eat, say, seven, and help them count these out.

• At the library, ask your child to choose, say, four, books. Let them count the books onto the librarian's desk.

• When you're going out, tell your child that they can choose two toys to take with them.

Children could throw balls of paper at a wastepaper basket and count how many went in and how many didn't.

One for you...

One of the main ideas children need to grasp as they begin to learn how to count is known as 'one-to-one correspondence'. This means matching one thing with another thing or person, such as a cookie for each person in the family, or one toy for each child. There are lots of everyday ways to help children understand this idea. On the left are two easy ones to try.

One-to-one

• Let children set the table. How many knives, forks and spoons will they need? Count 'One for Joe, one for Mom...'

• Cut a pizza or cake into slices and let your child put a slice on each plate to give to people. 'A piece for Dad, a piece for me...'

Activities with numbers

On the right there's an activity that provides another opportunity for young children to practice counting and to understand numbers as they cut and paste. If you use sheets of paper for the number pictures (instead of a notebook), you could stick them up on the wall, in order, to make a bedroom collage.

Going shopping with young children can be a more enjoyable experience for everybody if you play a few games as you travel, shop and unpack. Below are some number hunting ideas to try.

• In a store, set a task such as spotting a blue 4 or a red 3 on signs or packaging.

• Spot numbers in the street and on buses, cars, signs or billboards, on the way home.

• While you unpack, can your child find some numbers at home — on a clock, or phone, for example?

Lots of traditional children's games such as dominoes, ludo and hopscotch involve numbers and counting. There are more ideas for games that include numbers on page 62, and there are links to some good number games for children on the Usborne Quicklinks Website (see page 120).

Play a game with bowling pins made from plastic bottles half-filled with sand. Let children count how many they knock down each time they roll the ball.

1. Write the numbers 1 to 10 on separate sheets of paper or on the pages of a notebook.

2. Ask your child to find and cut out 'three pictures of flowers,' or 'four pictures of dogs' from magazines.

3. Ask them to stick the pictures on the correct sheet of paper or page for each number.

Who is heavier?

Let children weigh themselves and you on the scales at home.

Talk about who weighs the most. What happens if you both stand on the scales together?

All about measuring

Measuring things may not sound very exciting to you, but, for young children, it often is. They are very interested in who is bigger, heavier, or has the most. Whenever they pour water in the bathtub, try on shoes, or pack sand into buckets, they are finding out what words such as 'big', 'small', 'heavy' and 'full' mean. One of the main things children like to measure is themselves – how tall they are, how big their feet are and how high they can reach.

Getting bigger

It's easy to introduce young children to the idea of relative size (bigger than, smaller than, and so on) by bringing out a few of their baby and toddler shoes. Compare them with shoes that fit them now and talk about how much their feet have grown. Then add some of your own shoes and let the child put them all in size order.

Height charts are a great way for children to see and record how much they have grown over time. You can make one from several strips of paper or cardboard taped together, or from a long piece of wood. Let your child decorate the chart, if they want to, but leave one edge clear for measurements. Don't forget to mark the date on the chart as well as the child's height.

Jack 3-1-08

4 ft

Children like to see how they compare with friends and family.

1 m

3 ft

Comparing shoe sizes lets children see how they've grown – and how much they could still grow.

Baby Tom's shoe

Toddler Tom's shoe

Grown-up's shoe

Spoon, pour and stir

One of the best ways to give young children hands-on practice in measuring is to let them help you cook. Most will happily measure ingredients into cups and spoons. They will enjoy stirring, pouring, and scraping bowls even more. As they 'add a cup of flour' or 'break a large egg' they are learning about size and measuring in the best way possible, so try to make time to cook together. There are some good recipes to try on pages 90–93 of this book.

How many toys will fit into a toy buggy? Children may discover that they can squeeze in five small toys, but only three larger ones.

Children may like measuring toys with blocks; perhaps bunny is 'four blocks tall'? Many will enjoy experimenting with tape measures and rulers.

Help children measure ingredients, then let them try mixing and kneading, too.

My time

Young children often find it difficult to measure time, and they have very little idea what you mean when you say, 'Hurry up', or 'Five more minutes'. Even if they are too young to learn telling the time, it's good to help children realize that their time is divided up – by meals, by playtime and by bedtime, for instance. Try saying 'You must stop watching television when this program ends' or 'When this song finishes, it's time for bed' to help children measure time.

It's hard to understand that if you don't leave enough time to get somewhere, you'll be late...

Dominoes with dots, numbers or pictures to match are ideal for quieter times, as children need to concentrate to play.

Useful tip
Easy board games, such as snakes and ladders, or matching games such as memory or snap, help children learn numbers while they focus on winning the game.

Number games

Young children all over the world play games and sing songs and rhymes that include numbers and counting. These are not only fun – they're also one of the best ways of helping children learn to use numbers with confidence. Giving young children a good, enjoyable start in math is of enormous benefit to them in school, and in later life.

On this page are a few number games to try – some for outside, others for inside. You may need to make some a little easier for younger children, and some trickier for older ones – by adding a time limit, for instance. You'll find the words for several counting rhymes, and more ideas, on the Usborne Quicklinks Website (see page 120).

Children usually enjoy the rhythm and repetition in counting rhymes and it helps them to remember numbers.

• Teddy bear's picnic: Arrange some bears around a blanket. Put a bowl of dried pasta shapes in the middle and roll a dice to decide how many pieces each bear can have.

• Cushion count: See if a child can count up household things such as cushions or mirrors they can spot at home. They might need help if there are more than 10.

• Treasure hunt: Before a trip out, make a list of a few things for children to look for, and add simple pictures. Can they find 'five different leaves', or 'six flowers'?

My world

For young children, daily life brings so many new experiences that their days are rarely dull. This section of the book looks at their world – home, everyday life and the people that surround them – as a source of play ideas. Taking time to focus on these things will be even more valuable as they embark upon a whole new phase of their lives, at school.

My life

It's good for a child to realize that they live within a network of people — both family and friends.

Talking about what they do each day helps children learn about routine, and basic time-telling.

Any activity that makes children realize that they are unique is great for their self-confidence.

Most children are interested in their bodies and enjoy learning about them, and how to take care of them.

Useful tip

It's very important that children learn to say thank you for presents or small kindnesses other people show them.

Make this wall chart

1. On a large sheet of paper, ask the child to stick a photo or drawing of themselves in the middle. Let them try writing their name next to it.

2. Draw lines out to drawings or photos of parents, brothers, sisters, step-siblings and add their names. Don't forget pets, too.

3. Add other people who are important to the child, such as grandparents, cousins, nannies, babysitters, teachers and special friends.

Friends and family

When they begin visiting playgroups or enter day care or preschool, most children make new friends, but they probably still feel most secure with people who care for them on a regular basis. The ideas on these pages help you encourage young children to think about these important people in their lives, and how they feel about them.

Making a simple wall chart, using photos or drawings, helps children talk and think about all the special people in their lives. Start by talking together about who might be included, then follow the steps on the left, but try to leave most of the decision-making to them.

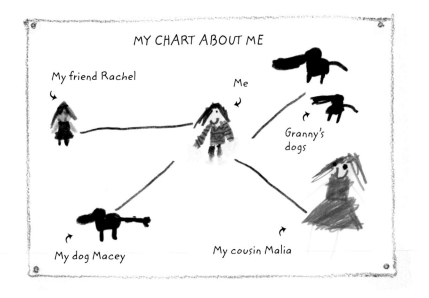

MY CHART ABOUT ME

My friend Rachel

Me

Granny's dogs

My dog Macey

My cousin Malia

Kind and caring

At home, among the family, is a very good place for young children to learn to be considerate of other people's feelings. Try these ideas to start with:

Young children like seeing how they fit into their family.

• If someone in the family is sick, ask a child to draw them a picture, or speak to them on the phone.

• Are there any toys or clothes you could both sort out and donate to a charity, for other children to enjoy?

• Tell them you appreciate their help if they get involved in putting away toys, or setting the table for dinner.

Feeling loved

Whatever your family is like, for a young child, it's the best in the world, and where they feel safest. It sounds simple, but it's really important to let children know they are loved. They need to know that even if you were very unhappy with them in the afternoon, they'll be forgiven with a hug by bedtime. Try to make sure you give your child plenty of praise, and if you say sorry when you are in the wrong, and teach them to do so too, they will learn that this is how a loving relationship works.

Don't forget to tell your children that you love them.

Happy days

Many children only see some family members on weekends, on vacation, or during holidays or special occasions. Encourage young children to talk about when they last saw their cousins or grandparents, for example. This helps them understand that they are still a part of these relatives' lives, even when they are not actually with them.

When children's behavior is exasperating, or you're tired, and you feel that all you do is scold them, remind yourself:

- All children misbehave from time to time.
- You are doing your best.
- Caring for young children is not always easy.
- Everyone makes mistakes.
- You love them.

Mommy and Auntie Jo

Me and Granny

Me and Auntie Sally

Spend some time looking at photos together of friends and family.

Children might enjoy making a scrapbook or collage of things from a special event, such as a wedding or a vacation. (Remember to help them collect some souvenirs at the time.) Whatever you do as a family, helping children see that they are part of the activities gives them a real sense of belonging.

Children could add to their scrapbook with some pictures or words of their own.

You can often pick up on the way children feel by watching how they move.

Faces and bodies

Young children experience lots of different emotions every day, and they usually express them in the way they behave, or move their bodies. They may surprise you with their sensitivity, too, and will often pick up on your moods. Helping them find out about their body and how it works, and their feelings, is very important. There are some ideas to help you on these pages.

I can do that!

By the age of about three, many children can kick and catch a large, soft ball, balance on one foot, jump, climb up stairs and run. They are interested in what their body can do, and are always eager to try to do even more. Ask them to negotiate an obstacle course on a tricycle, or while walking backward, or spend some time throwing and catching different-sized balls. Set them small, physical challenges – but keep it fun, and safe.

This may be a good time to introduce children to the idea that we all have different skills and talents. Perhaps Thomas can run the fastest, but Molly is excellent at riding a tricycle, for example. It's especially valuable for children to grasp this idea if they find it hard not to win, or be the best in every game they play – as many do.

Children soon learn that to be good at something usually takes a lot of practice.

Playing with others gives children the chance to explore what they can do – or try something new!

Take care of yourself

Young children are usually very aware when their body doesn't feel right and they are unwell. Encourage them to understand their body's messages. If they're cold, suggest they put on warm clothes. If their tummy hurts, could those cookies be to blame? Help them learn to respect and respond to their body – and stay healthy. Ensuring basic levels of hygiene can be a struggle at times, but below are some ideas to help make it all a little more enjoyable.

I brushed my teeth		
Sunday		
Monday		
Tuesday		
Wednesday		
Thursday		
Friday		
Saturday		

Make a simple star chart for each job done: five stars, perhaps, wins a small prize.

To encourage hand-washing after using the toilet, provide a liquid soap (one that you can smell when it has been used).

If your child hates bathing or showering, invest in a jazzy shower cap, or some glittery or fruity bubble bath.

There's a wide choice of novelty toothbrushes available that may encourage children to brush their teeth.

Useful tip
Young children don't know that it's rude to stare at someone who looks 'different'. If they do so, gently tell them to stop. Later, explain that staring can hurt people's feelings.

How would you feel?

An awareness of people's differences, as well as how they are alike, helps children grow in kindness and tolerance, which can only be good. These activities are easy, everyday ways of extending their, usually natural, instinct to be kind.

• Spend a while looking at people's faces in a book or magazine and let children interpret how those people might be feeling.

• Talk about how to behave in situations (such as if someone is sick) and why. This will help children learn how to manage their feelings.

• Make sure children know that there are all sorts of different people in the world, of varying age, color, size, beliefs and lifestyles.

• Be open about your own feelings whenever you can so that children understand that at times everyone feels sad, happy, angry and so on.

If you can, choose quiet, calm moments in the day to talk about feelings.

At home

Life can be hectic for young children, and many have long days away from home. This makes it even more important for them to be able to relax afterward. One of the most important things about being at home for a child is that they can choose what to do, rather than following a strict schedule. When they get home, let them play with toys, listen to music, draw or watch a favorite television program for a while before starting any new activity.

Young children often need some quiet time to relax when they get home after a busy day.

Daily patterns

Although home is not like preschool or day care, it can help you both to have some pattern if you spend whole days at home. You don't need a rigid routine, but some ground rules, such as 'We get dressed after breakfast', may help. Being consistent in what you ask of them makes children feel more secure (and your life much easier).

'My week' poster

1. Divide a large sheet of paper into seven wide rows. Let the child write (or tell you to write) the days of the week on the left of each one.

2. Write down what the child does each day. Suggest they draw a picture to go with, perhaps, 'going to Grandma's for the night on Saturday'.

3. If your child asks you 'Where am I going today?', point to the right day on the poster, where they can see what the day will hold.

My week	
Sunday	Soccer
Monday	Buy present for Joe
Tuesday	Art club
Wednesday	
Thursday	Joe's Party
Friday	Sleepover at Grandma's house
Saturday	

Young children often like to know what's going to happen each day and this can also help them to feel secure. You can show them, and help them learn the days of the week, by making a 'My week' poster to put up at home. Just follow the simple steps on the left.

Room by room

Home is the most familiar place in the world to a child, so it's a good starting point for several guessing games and activities. Here are some to try:

• To improve their memory skills, ask your child to tell you five things in each room of your home (without looking).

• Can your child tell you two things that your family does in each room, such as eating, sleeping, bathing or playing?

• Choose a room and see if your child can guess which it is by asking you questions, such as 'Do I sleep there?'.

• Select a household item, such as a refrigerator or sofa, and see if your child can tell you which room it belongs in.

Follow my trail:

1. Walk around a room in your home trailing a long piece of string.

2. Can your child follow your trail, winding the string into a ball after you?

Home comforts

It's good to talk to young children about all kinds of homes. Not everyone has a yard, for example, and everyone's home is different. You could look at books about homes around the world and talk about what a home needs – somewhere to cook, eat, sleep, bathe and use the toilet. Older children might enjoy drawing a basic layout of a home. Younger ones could just draw the room they sleep in.

Children could cut out shapes or pictures to add to the drawing.

Useful tip

You may find that young children want to talk about what goes on in the bathroom. This is natural, so don't worry about it.

Walk and talk

• Talk about the things you pass on a walk. Encourage children to think about what they hear, smell or see.

• Play spotting games, such as 'Who can spot a yellow flower or red car first?'

• Make up a silly routine, such as three big steps, a small one and a hop, together.

Children often need to be reminded to concentrate whenever they cross a road.

Where I live

For young children, the world is very much centered around where they live, whether it's on a busy city street or a quiet country lane. The area they live in is full of places to explore, things to ask questions about and people who form part of their daily life.

Take a trip

The best way for children to get to know their area is to let them see it first-hand, at their own pace. Walk rather than drive whenever you can, as children notice much more if they are given the time and opportunity. Older children might be interested in talking about buildings you pass, younger ones may just be pleased to see the mail carrier.

If you draw a very simple plan of the route you've taken at home, children could add things they've seen to it. Some enjoy remembering the route by saying it aloud: 'Then we go past the post office, over the railroad track, past the man selling papers and there's the school.' This develops their observation and memory skills.

Road safety

Even though young children should never be alone anywhere near a road, it's important to show them how to cross roads safely. Make sure you hold your child's hand whenever you are about to cross, and encourage them to follow these steps with you:

1. Find a safe place to cross where you can see clearly.

2. Stop at the curb. Listen. Look both ways and then again.

3. If you are sure there is nothing approaching, cross the road.

4. Keep looking and listening while you are crossing.

The world around me

Most young children are intensely curious about nature, and enjoy finding out about animals, birds, plants or bugs. It's important to help children understand that they are only one of the many living things that share the Earth. The ideas in this section encourage their interest, stimulate their senses and help them learn to value the world around them.

Making a nature lover

Caring for plants and animals helps children be responsible, and remember others' needs.

Watching living things shows them the cycle of life — birth, raising young, and death.

Exploring the world around them helps develop early observation and scientific skills.

While children are outdoors, they will be getting lots of fresh air and exercise, too.

Mini-gardeners

You don't need a garden for young children to grow things. There are many other ways of giving them the pleasure of seeing something they have planted, and cared for, begin to grow. Even if you have no previous experience of gardening, here are some ways for you both to see things grow.

A walk in the park

One good way of encouraging young children to notice things growing around them is to go on a nature walk together. There are some tips to get you started on the left. Ideally, try a trip to a park or a green space, but even a street in a town may have something living and growing, somewhere, if you both look hard enough. If you can, revisit these places at different times of the year and see if you can spot any changes – flowers in bloom or leaves changing color, for instance.

Nature walk

1. Take a container to collect interesting things such as leaves or shells.

2. Talk as you walk, answering children's questions about what you see as best you can.

3. Let children lift stones, touch bark or smell flowers, but not eat, hurt or damage things.

4. At home, talk about the things you have collected and about where you found them.

5. Don't forget everyone needs to wash their hands afterward (and explain to children why).

Useful tip

Looking at pits or seeds in fruit can help children grasp the idea that big things grow from tiny ones.

Blowing on a dandelion seedhead helps children see how its seeds are scattered.

What can we grow?

Children can learn a lot from growing things whether in a garden or on a balcony or windowsill. As children watch seeds sprout or flowers bloom, they see that plants need care, water, sunlight and space to grow well; and if the plants don't get these things, they don't thrive. On the right are some suggestions for plants that are fairly easy for young children to grow.

Cress — Help children spread a layer of damp kitchen paper towels in a clean container such as a margarine tub. Sprinkle on cress seeds, put the tub on a windowsill and keep the seeds moist.

Cherry tomatoes — Buy some cherry tomato plants in late spring and help children plant them in a growing bag outside. Water regularly and feed with tomato plant food. Pick the tomatoes when they are red.

Sunflowers — Buy sunflower seeds from a garden store. Fill a plant pot with compost and plant seeds 2 ½ inches deep. Water regularly and transfer seedlings to bigger pots or plant outside as they grow.

Children will be amazed at how a tall sunflower plant can grow from a little seed.

Tiny garden

This activity gives children the chance to design a mini-garden on an old tray or baking tray. They will also need some silver foil and compost or garden soil to get started:

Old tray

Half an eggshell

Twig tree

1. Line the tray with aluminum foil. Help the child collect moss, leaves, twigs, pebbles, shells, flowers and other small things, such as little toys.

2. Sprinkle compost or garden soil over the foil. A circle of foil kept soil-free makes a shiny pond, or your child could fill half an eggshell with water.

3. Let children design their mini-garden. It may have stone paths, twig trees, a pebbly patio, or flowers floating in eggshell ponds.

Don't forget to talk to your child about their mini-garden and ask them all about it.

Catching bugs

1. You'll need a clear glass or plastic container, a cup, some clingfilm, a rubber band and a piece of thin cardboard.

2. Let your child put some soil, leaves, grass and twigs in the container so the bugs will have food, moisture and somewhere to hide.

3. When you spot a bug, put the cup over it. Gently slide the cardboard underneath, then gently drop the creature into the container.

4. Cover the container with clingfilm, secure with the rubber band and make air holes. Let children watch the bug for a day or so before setting it free.

Animal-lovers

Although many young children are interested in animals, many are, understandably, nervous about being near them. You don't need to own a pet, live on a farm, or visit a zoo to introduce children to animals. There are some easy ways to help them find out more about how animals live and behave, and some tips on overcoming their possible fears, on these pages.

Start small

Although many young children live with pets, and gain from the experience, owning a pet can bring responsibilities that are too great for children to fulfil on their own, and it may not suit your family, or lifestyle. If you are caring for a child who is desperate to get near some real, live animals, try starting small. You could take care of some bugs, such as caterpillars or beetles, for a while. Find out how to catch them safely on the left. (It's best to avoid catching spiders, as they may eat any other bugs you catch.)

Teach children how to pick up and handle animals gently.

Tell me about...

Seeing more unusual animals in real life can be valuable, so a trip to a zoo, wildlife park or farm may be a great day out, especially as many have all kinds of hands-on activities and play areas for young children. If you have time, find out and talk about the animals you may see before you go, using the ideas on the right.

• Help your child find books about their favorite animals at a library or bookstore.

• If you have a computer, search for pictures of the animals your child likes best.

• Find out where the animals live, what they eat and how they care for their young.

Try letting children explore the sights, sounds and smells at a local farm.

Safety point

Everybody should wash their hands thoroughly after touching animals and before eating or drinking to minimize the risk of bacterial infections.

I'm scared

Many preschools and kindergartens have wormeries, tadpoles or stick insects in tanks, or a hamster in a cage. The children can take turns taking care of these animals during holidays or vacations. Such experiences are ideal, short-term ways of giving children confidence in being around living creatures and in caring for them. Offering to help feed, groom or walk friends' pets from time to time may help a young child who is unsure about animals. Try to remember that if *you* feel uncomfortable around dogs or hate spiders, children pick up on it, so try to keep your feelings under control, if you can.

Taking care of a friend's pet while they're away can be a learning opportunity.

Weather-watching

Young children start each day ready to play and explore, whatever the weather. The main effect weather has on them is what clothes they need to put on. Despite this, many children are naturally interested in changes in the weather, and are interested in finding out more about it.

What shall we wear?

Most preschools and day cares emphasize the importance of wearing the right clothes for the day's weather. They make sure children put on coats for outdoor play on chilly days, raincoats and boots on wet days, and sun hats and sunscreen when it's hot. This helps children understand what the weather means to them, so it's a good idea to do the same at home, and give children the chance to think and talk about what to wear each day.

Talk to children about why they need to wear a sun hat and sunscreen on sunny days — so they don't get sunburned.

Weather art activities

• *Provide some dark paper and let children glue on cotton balls, rice grains or powdered sugar to create snowy pictures.*

• *Chalks are perfect for creating murky, rainy or foggy pictures, especially when rubbed with fingers.*

• *Get children to draw, color and cut out weather images, such as clouds, suns, snowflakes or rainbows. Hang them from a wire coat hanger as a mobile or make a weather scrapbook.*

Children might enjoy a weather-based game called 'What shall we take?' Start by explaining it is only a game (in case they think you're both heading off somewhere, when you aren't). Then ask, for example, 'It's hot – let's go to the beach. What shall we take?' or 'Let's go for a walk in the woods. What shall we take?' If you pretend to put things into a bag, it saves a putting-away marathon later.

What weather does

Many children are more interested in what weather does than what it is. When the wind takes a child's kite soaring, or the rain gives their tricycle a bath, it makes weather real to them. The simple experiments on the right show the weather in action.

Even young children can begin to understand that the world's weather is changing and that what people do can affect it, if you talk to them about it. You could buy or borrow books to help you explain more about how the weather works, or look at the Usborne Quicklinks Website (see page 120).

Weather experiments

• In really cold weather, fill a plastic bottle with water and leave it outside overnight. Children will see that water 'gets bigger' when it freezes.

• In hot weather, let your child paint water pictures on the sidewalk, a wall or paper. Soon the pictures will be gone, dried up by the sun.

• Collect rainwater in plastic containers. This is a good, clear way of showing children how much rain has fallen. Use it to water plants.

Flying a kite on a windy day gives children the chance to feel just how strong the wind can be.

Useful tip

Try to let children go outside every day so long as the weather is safe. If their clothes are suitable, no weather is bad weather for young children.

The seasons

A year is a very long time to young children. They may know that different things happen at different times, such as going on vacation or celebrating their birthday, but most need help to become aware of the passing of the seasons. This can be done in small, everyday ways, such as by going outside regularly to see what's changed, or by taking photographs of the same tree or flowerbed at different times of year and comparing them.

• In spring, point out new leaves and plant shoots.

• In summer, look for flowers and blossom trees.

• In the fall, collect fallen leaves and compare colors.

• In winter, put out food and water for hungry birds.

Talk to children about falling leaves and other seasonal changes.

Your child could make a nature scrapbook, sticking in things such as dried leaves to remind them of different seasons.

What does it remind you of?

Each time of the year has its own smell. It may be that of a grill, cut grass or a smoky bonfire, but smell is a powerful memory-jogger. What you use for this activity depends on what happens in your house during the year, and what festivals you celebrate, but here's how it works:

1. Explain that you are going to play a game in which they don't need to guess what they are smelling, just what it reminds them of.

2. Put, for example, a blob of sunscreen, a pinch of wintry spices (ginger and cinnamon) or some orange peel on separate plates.

3. Cover the child's eyes and ask them to smell the things on the plates. What do they make them think of? Do they bring back any memories?

Useful tip

Children like things that happen regularly. If you can, build some seasonal activities into your family's year — pecan hunting in the fall, for instance.

Active play

It is very important for young children to have the opportunity to run, jump, skip, hop and kick a ball as often as possible. Giving them the chance to enjoy daily active play not only aids their physical development and helps them to stay healthy, it may help combat health problems as they grow older, too. This part of the book gives lots of ideas for getting young children moving, both indoors and outdoors.

Mini-movers

Children need lots of chances to be able to move their bodies freely and confidently.

To be fit and healthy, children need a balance of physical play and more gentle activities.

Energetic play often involves interacting with other children, which develops social skills.

Children learn coordination skills through active games, and how to follow simple rules.

Active play helps them master skills such as balancing, jumping, running and climbing.

Indoor games

Experts recommend that children get at least an hour of active play a day. On these pages you'll find suggestions for energetic activities for days when going outdoors isn't possible. Just be prepared for a little furniture-rearranging – and some noise.

As a child's brain develops, so does their body's ability to do things, and whatever kinds of active play you set up, children will enjoy seeing what they can do, using their imaginations to try things out, and getting used to how exercise feels. Playing at home also gives less confident children the chance to try things out with you, and lessens the risk of their feeling not as confident as others when they come to play games or take PE at school.

See if your child can walk on their hands while you hold onto their ankles.

Encourage children to walk along a string or rope tightrope on the floor.

Set up a limbo bar by balancing a pole or cane between pieces of furniture.

A children's activity ball, (or an adult's fitness ball) is ideal for indoor games and encourages children to move and stretch.

Safety point

Indoor active play can get boisterous, so remember to keep a careful watch on children at all times.

If you have space, children could try playing with hula hoops, activity balls or jump ropes indoors. They may enjoy a game of indoor volleyball with a balloon or a soft ball made from a sock filled with scrunched-up paper. You could make tunnels for children to crawl through by putting chairs in a row and draping blankets over them. There are some more ideas to try on the left.

Indoor work-out

Few homes are spacious enough to set up an indoor gym for an energetic preschool child, but on the right are some ways of making the most of whatever space you have.

Young children often enjoy moving to music. Encourage them to stretch up, skip and do jumping jacks.

Circuit challenge

Setting up the following activity takes a little time, but you can play it many times once you have established the routine. Remember that the main goal of the game is to get children moving.

Useful tip

Children often get anxious about things they can't do, so keep things relaxed and fun, encourage your child, and try not to expect too much from them.

Hop 7 times
Do 2 twists
Do 10 jumps
Do 10 bends

1. Write a few active tasks, such as 'Hop 7 times', or 'Do 10 jumps' onto separate pieces of paper. Put each piece in a different place.

2. Explain to your child that they need to do a different thing in each place. Help them to read the tasks so they know exactly what they'll have to do.

3. Now let them do the circuit on their own. How fast can they do it? Can they do it in reverse order? You could make the tasks a little harder.

Scooters and tricycles get children moving and help balance and coordination.

Outdoor games

Most young children love nothing more than being allowed to run free in a large, open space. Their growing bodies need to move, and it's far easier for them to burn off some of their energy outdoors. If you can, visit an outdoor space as often as possible with young children. Their general health, eating and sleeping habits should all benefit from active play outside.

The overwhelming tiredness that can accompany caring for young children may make being active the last thing on your mind. But, if you are going to establish healthy habits in a child's life, it's important to try to set a good example now, bearing in mind the tips below, on the left.

Setting a good example

• If you can, build a regular time for active, physical play into your daily routine. Mid-morning is a good slot.

• Walk whenever you can. You may need to allow more time, but you'll find you talk and see more together.

• Overall, try to show children that being active is a good thing (even if you haven't enjoyed it before).

Swings, slides and seesaws

Remember that many parks have a safe, well-planned play area for young children, where they can use play equipment such as swings, slides and seesaws. You could also find out if there are any nature trails or activity classes at a local park. Visit your local library, or contact your parks department, to find out what's on offer.

Children find all kinds of ways of playing with outdoor equipment.

Playing together

Young children need to learn about winning and losing, but this should be done gradually, and with kindness. If you feel that races and competitive activities are not fun, just leave them. Playing games in teams is very valuable for young children, however. It helps them learn to cooperate with each other and be considerate.

You may want to adapt these games slightly according to the age and physical confidence of the children. You only need some basic equipment.

Lay a board or rope on the ground for walking along.

Make an area for jogging, and jumping or hopping on one foot.

• The children need to stand in a line about 3 feet apart. Let them try throwing a big, soft ball to each other.

• Ask the children to hold hands. You are 'it'. How many children can you catch? They need to run together to escape.

• Make two goalposts (coats on the grass will do). You're the goalkeeper. How many goals can the children's team score?

There are some more outdoor play activities to try on the right. Whatever activities you set up, stay close by, and make sure no child feels they have to do something they can't, or don't want to.

Set up low hurdles, by tying some string between chairs.

Useful tip
Children know that you value their efforts if you're cheering at the finish line — even if they're last.

Swimming

There are some very good reasons for taking young children swimming. It gives them an awareness of what to do in water and will make them safer whenever they are in, or around, it. It's also enjoyable for them, and good exercise, using lots of different muscles.

Just as when they were babies or toddlers, taking young children swimming needs a little planning. You may not need to think about swim diapers any more, but it's a good idea to bear the guidelines on the left in mind.

Safety point

Never leave young children alone in, or near, water, even wading in the ocean. Accidents only take seconds.

Swimming guidelines

• Try to choose a time when the pool is not too busy.

• Don't plan to swim if your child is tired, or sick.

• Wait an hour after a meal before going swimming.

• Stay in the children's pool or at the shallow end of a big one while your child is learning to swim.

• It's better to go often, for a short time, than for a few long sessions.

Water skills

Young children can learn to float, turn, stretch and move in water long before they master any strokes. Blowing bubbles and getting safely in and out of the water are useful skills to master, too. Always take things at your child's pace, and stop if they have had enough or seem to be getting too tired, or cold.

Flotation aids can help to build a child's confidence in the water.

Staying afloat

Flotation aids such as armbands, arm discs, noodles and swimsuits with slot-in buoyancy blocks give children the chance to move their arms and kick their legs freely in the water. They will not stop a child from drowning, however; and you must stay close by, and watch them at all times. If you aren't sure how to use a flotation aid, a member of the pool staff may be able to help. They should be able to show you how each type works.

At this stage, making sure your child has fun should be your priority; there's plenty of time for swimming lessons later. Try to develop confidence in the water as much as you can. If your child seems happy, introduce some play time without flotation aids, making sure you always provide support. This is how your child will start to feel confident in the water.

Water activities

- *Encourage children to jump in. Make sure you're in the water to catch them and guide them back to the pool side.*

- *Give children a float to hold out in front of them while they kick their legs to reach some 'treasure' (small floating toys).*

- *Some children enjoy putting their heads under water; others aren't so willing. To begin with, just show your child how to blow bubbles in the water.*

- *Standing in a little from the pool side, encourage the child to push off from the side and glide to you through the water.*

- *Do some action rhymes in shallow water. Try 'Ring-a-Round-the-Rosies' while holding hands and turning in a circle.*

These flotation aids are all suitable for young children.

Arm discs

Buoyancy belt

Noodle

Water fears

Some young children are frightened of going into the water and need lots of encouragement. Never make a fearful child do anything that they are unhappy to do. Remember that swimming is an important life skill: your patience and kindness now may make the difference between a child overcoming their fears, or having to live with them for years.

Useful tip

Take a healthy snack and drink with you for after the swim session, when you will probably all be hungry.

Happy and healthy

What parents and caregivers want above all is for the children they love to be happy and healthy. Here are a few basic things that are worth remembering.

It's all about balance

Of course, children need to be loved and cared for to be happy, but they also need variety in how they play, as this is how they learn. Give them plenty of opportunities to play, in lots of different ways. Strive for each day to include a balance of active, energetic activities and quieter, more thoughtful ones.

The food children eat should give them a balanced diet. Your child's doctor or a dietician can you guidance on what that should be if you are unsure, but remember that the eating habits they adopt now may last a lifetime. There's more about food and cooking with children in the next section of this book.

Learning from you

Without expecting yourself to be perfect, try to set as good an example as you can. Children learn a lot from what they see around them. Try to be active regularly, to walk and talk together, and to eat healthy yourself. It may help you to remember that *your* lifestyle is the one children will see, share and learn from.

Useful tip
It's easy to cram too much into a young child's day. Try to make time for simple things, such as snuggling up on the sofa.

For a young child, spending some time with you is usually what makes them happiest.

Children need quiet time, just to relax and unwind.

Food and cooking

For adults, food and cooking are often
a source of great pleasure. Young children don't
always feel like this, however, and many parents
and caregivers worry about what and how much
children eat. This section of the book gives you some
tips for helping children enjoy food and eat well.
There are some recipes to make together, too.

Finding out about food

Diet really does affect a child's growth, behavior,
learning and development.

Eating healthy now will make children
healthier grown-ups.

Children are more likely to eat good food if they
have helped grow, prepare or cook it.

Cooking teaches children useful skills, such as how to cut,
measure, stir, and follow steps in a recipe.

Can we cook?

It can be tempting to answer 'Not today', to this question. Life is too busy to cook with a young child every day, so just try to do it whenever you can. As experts worry about rises in childhood obesity, allergies, hyperactivity and troublesome behavior, which may be linked to the kinds of food children eat, getting them interested in cooking and food is more important than ever.

The whole process

For children, cooking is an experience that they can't have without your help. Involve them in the whole process by choosing a recipe together, making (or drawing) a list of ingredients you will need and going shopping for them, if necessary. Also make sure children help with the cleaning up and washing dishes as much as they can. When the food is ready, let them show it off to family and friends before eating it.

Useful tip
Most boys enjoy cooking as much as girls do. Don't forget to let them try.

Look at some children's cook-books together or use one of the recipes in this book. Choose one you feel your child can do, and will enjoy eating.

Explain the rules everyone needs to follow. Wash hands, tie back hair and put aprons on. Keep children away from sharp knives and hot things.

Help children measure the ingredients using measuring cups and spoons. They can learn a lot as they measure, pour and spoon.

You'll need to show children how to do some steps in a recipe, but let them do as much as possible themselves.

'I don't like it'

Eating is far from straightforward for some children. For people who care for them, preparing a meal only to have to throw it away when they refuse to eat it yet again is disheartening and worrying, as children need to eat.

This anxiety makes it tempting to offer children things you know they will eat – however unhealthy – rather than risk a tantrum. This in turn sends the child the message that they have 'won' – and may encourage them to refuse the next meal, too. If you are having problems in this area, try the tips on the right. Experts agree that children are very unlikely to starve themselves. When they do eat, or try something new, praise them, and take comfort from the fact that most picky eaters get better.

Dealing with picky eaters

• Limit between-meal snacks. Keep them small, and healthy.

• Whenever you can, let your child help you to prepare their food.

• Eat with your child, or invite a friend or relative along to eat.

• If they won't eat, say nothing – but offer nothing else either.

• Set a good example. Eat well and try to make mealtimes sociable.

• Talk about healthy food and why our bodies need it.

• If you're really worried, ask your child's doctor for advice.

Research shows that children may need to try a new food up to ten times before deciding they like it, so don't give up on offering new tastes.

What kind of food?

It's a good idea to give children the chance to enjoy as many different kinds of food as you can from an early age so they get used to different flavors, textures and colors. Getting them to like the healthy part of the meal as well as treats is important too. It's smart to offer desserts and sweet things as a treat, so that kids get used to eating healthy things.

Useful tip
You could offer children cut up raw vegetables, such as carrot sticks, while you are getting a meal ready. These won't spoil their appetite.

Main courses

Letting young children help cook a family meal gives them a great sense of achievement and it's also an ideal time to talk about different kinds of food and why we need to eat them. The recipes here are simple to make. Younger children may need more help than older ones, of course.

Pasta and vegetable sauce

This recipe uses passata (tomato sauce with vegetables). You could serve the pasta with a big mixed salad (see right).

1. Help children peel the onion and wipe and slice the mushrooms. Cut the onion and pepper into little pieces.
2. Heat the oil in a saucepan and cook the onion until see-through. Add the mushrooms, garlic and pepper and cook until soft and brown. Take the pan off the heat.
3. After five minutes, let children stir in the tomato sauce. Let them pour the dried pasta into a bowl.
4. Put the sauce back on the heat with its lid on, and let it simmer while you boil water, cook and drain the pasta.
5. Help children grate the cheese. Put some pasta, then sauce into bowls. Children can add a sprinkling of cheese.

Ingredients for
Pasta and vegetable sauce
(serves 4)

- 1 large onion
- 8 button mushrooms
- 1 red pepper (deseeded)
- a little olive oil for frying
- 1 clove of garlic (crushed) or ¹/₂ tablespoon minced garlic
- one 14 oz. can tomato sauce
- 4 oz. dried pasta for each adult, 2 oz. for each child
- (¹/₂ cup) cheddar or or Parmesan

Safety points

Keep a very close eye on children at all times in the kitchen and keep them away from the oven, hot pans, sharp kitchen tools and hot liquids.

You could let little children pretend to cook with water and dried pasta.

Salads, pittas, pizzas, potatoes

Salads are healthy and easy to make. Choose a few of the ingredients below, then help children prepare, and arrange the salad in a bowl. On the right are more ways of letting children assemble their own meals.

Let children stuff their own pitta bread with a spoonful of hummus and some salad.

Helping to make a salad may make a child more willing to eat it.

Let children spread tomato sauce over a pizza crust and arrange tasty things on top before you cook it.

Bake potatoes in a hot oven for about 1 hour. Cut open and fluff with a fork. Let children add butter and grated cheese.

Salad ideas:
- Lettuce, salad leaves or spinach
- Cherry tomato halves
- Cucumber (sliced or cubed)
- Alfalfa sprouts or beansprouts
- Green onions (sliced)
- Raw carrot (grated)
- Orange segments, raisins or chopped apple
- Chopped avocado
- Cubes of hard cheese
- Canned corn
- Cold, cooked potatoes (sliced, or cubed)
- Chopped red, yellow or orange pepper
- Canned beans, such as chickpeas, butter beans or kidney beans

Kebabs

Children often enjoy helping to thread food onto skewers to make kebabs. You can make these with cubed meat or tofu, or chunks of onion, pepper, zucchini, pineapple and cherry tomatoes. Grill meat kebabs for about 5 minutes on each side, until cooked. Cook vegetable kebabs until they start to soften and brown. Serve with salad in pitta bread.

Useful tip
Use wooden skewers and soak them in water before use to stop them from burning. (It's safer not to use metal ones, which get very hot.)

Sweet recipes

Most children love sweet foods, and cakes, cookies and desserts are among the most satisfying things to make. Remember to keep sugary things just for treats, though, as too many are not good for anyone's health, or teeth. Here are some easy, sweet recipes for you to make together.

Many children enjoy the tasks involved with baking.

Safety point

Don't let children lick spoons or bowls when a mixture contains raw egg. Eggs can be a source of salmonella bacteria that can cause food poisoning.

Little sponge cupcakes

This recipe makes about 12 small cupcakes that children will enjoy decorating with icing and candies.

1. Preheat the oven to 350°F.
2. Help your child beat the margarine and sugar together in a bowl, until the mixture is soft and creamy.
3. Crack the eggs into a cup and let your child beat them with a fork. Ask your child to stir the egg bit by bit into the mixture. Don't worry if it gets a little lumpy.
4. Help your child stir the flour gently into the mixture a spoonful at a time.
5. Ask your child to put the baking cups into a muffin tray or onto a baking sheet.
6. Help your child spoon about two tablespoonfuls of mixture into each of the paper cups.
7. Bake the cupcakes for 10 minutes or until risen and brown. Leave them to cool on a wire rack.
8. Add drops of milk to the powedered sugar until it's like melted chocolate and let your child decorate the cupcakes.

Ingredients for Little sponge cupcakes
- $^2/_3$ cup sugar
- 8 tablespoons (1 stick) soft margarine
- 4 eggs
- 1 cup self-rising flour (sifted)
- 12 paper baking cups
- $^3/_4$ cup powdered sugar
- 12 small candies

Put a candy on top

Let children spread a little icing on top of each cupcake. It doesn't matter how messy they look.

Pancakes

Pancakes, like bread, are slightly different around the world, and toppings vary too. Maple syrup, lemon juice, stewed fruit, ice cream or chopped fresh fruit and whipped cream are a few possibilities. Children will enjoy beating the pancake batter, but you must do the actual cooking.

1. Let children sift the dry ingredients into a bowl, and make a 'well' in it using a spoon.
2. You crack the egg into the well. Your child can stir.
3. Pour in the milk, a little at a time, as your child beats.
4. Mix until the batter is smooth.
5. Heat a teaspoon of oil in a frying pan or preheated griddle. Pour a little batter into the pan to cover it. Cook until edges are firm and bubbles appear on the top.
6. Flip the pancake over with a spatula to cook the other side.
7. Slide the pancake onto a plate. Let children add whichever topping you provide.

Ingredients

- ¹/₄ teaspoon baking powder
- ¹/₂ teaspoon baking soda
- ¹/₄ teaspoon salt
- 1 ¹/₂ teaspoons sugar
- 1 cup milk
- 1 cup flour
- 1 egg, beaten

Useful tip

There is a lot of sugar in sodas. Try to give young children water, low-fat milk or diluted fruit juice, instead.

Fruit fans

Fresh fruit is a good, natural source of sugar. Encourage children to eat as many different kinds as possible, including some more unusual ones. If you help with peeling and chopping, children may enjoy making a fruit salad. As a treat, melt a bar of chocolate in a heatproof bowl over a pan of boiling water – dark chocolate, with a high cocoa content, is healthiest. Using a fork, dip pieces of fruit into the chocolate. Strawberries are especially delicious, but make sure the chocolate cools down before children eat it.

To make a smoothie, blend some fruit and plain yogurt or apple juice in a blender.

Party food

A birthday or holiday party is a very special occasion for young children, but few of them are really bothered about the food. You don't need to stay up all night making mouth-watering food – you deserve to enjoy the day, too. If you like baking, you could make a birthday cake, but your child may be just as happy with a store-bought one.

It's important to keep a balance between the healthy snacks and sweet foods. If you fill ten preschool children with sugary food and carbonated drinks, they may well become hyperactive, and ruin your party plans. Put the healthy food out on the table first, and don't produce any sweet stuff until you're sure they've eaten some of it.

In general, keep things simple and don't over-cater. Young children are rarely big eaters, and would much rather play party games than sit at a table. On the left are some ideas for food that's easy to prepare, and should be popular.

Healthy party food:

- Little sandwiches
- Squares of pizza (check if any guests are vegetarian)
- Bowls of hummus with cut-up raw carrots, celery and peppers
- Crackers topped with cheese or hard-boiled egg slices
- Bowls of plain popcorn (microwave popcorn is easy)
- Cherry tomato halves
- A variety of reduced-fat and salt snack mixes and nuts

Sweet party treats:

- Ice cream
- Bowls of strawberries, orange segments, grapes or raisins
- Muffins, cupcakes or cookies
- Some chocolate treats (at the end)

Useful tip

It's always a good idea to check if any of your guests are allergic to certain things before you plan your party food.

Active minds

For a lot of their day, young children are constantly investigating, asking questions, trying out ideas, or seeing if they can solve problems. Some experts call this area of their learning 'extending their knowledge and understanding of the world', but it can also be called simple first science. This part of the book has ideas for satisfying children's curiosity about how the world works, and answering a few of those questions.

How and why?

Finding out about the world around them helps children learn vital skills, such as thinking and problem solving.

They can discover how, and why, some things happen.

Children's natural curiosity is amazing and, when encouraged, it can help them make sense of the world.

They learn some of the basic rules of science.

Children need to try out ideas; some will work, others won't, and that's fine.

Young scientists

You don't need test tubes, microscopes or expert knowledge to help young children have their first taste of science. It's all around us, every day, and most children are naturally interested in finding out about how things work. One of the very best ways of encouraging them is to let them ask questions, and find things out for themselves. You could answer some of the questions, but it's fine to say 'I don't know – we should find out,' to some of the others.

What happens when...?

Young children can learn a lot about substances, and what they do by playing with water. Help them use words such as 'freeze', 'melt', 'float', 'sink' and 'dissolve'. Put newspaper on the floor in case of spills, and dress children in aprons or old clothes.

Pools and sandboxes

Most young children will still enjoy playing with wading pools and sandboxes. Let them experiment with scooping up water in different containers, or watching it trickle through the holes in a sieve, for example. 'Fishing' with a magnet for small metal objects buried in the sand often works well, too. Such simple, experimental play is very valuable.

Water experiments

• Fill a sink with water and let children see what floats (a toy boat, a plastic bowl) and what sinks (a stone, a key). What happens to things with holes.

• Fill containers with water and let children add drops of different food coloring. Mix them together, too, and see what new colors form.

• What happens when children put layers of vegetable oil and colored water into a plastic bottle? Then put on the lid and shake the bottle...

• Let children stir some sugar into a cup of water, or add some bath salts to their bath. What do they think happens to the grains in the liquid?

Look at this

Food provides lots of easy ways of introducing children to how different materials feel, change and behave. They don't need to understand the scientific processes, or words, to find them interesting. Try the ideas on the right. There are some more on the Usborne Quicklinks Website (see page 120).

Show children how chocolate melts when warmed, but turns into a solid again when cool.

Push and pull

The idea of explaining scientific forces (such as pushing and pulling) may sound pretty scary, but children are using them every day – when they make a swing move, pull the brake on a bike, squeeze dough or watch the wind take a kite into the sky. Just draw attention to these things and they'll learn about them.

Leave some bread or fruit to go moldy. Children will find the changes fascinating (but mustn't touch the mold).

Whenever you can, help children think about their effect on things, too – 'when you push your bike pedal, it goes around'. The concept of cause and effect takes some time to grasp, but helping children see science in their daily life makes things interesting, relevant and easier to understand.

Corn changes dramatically when it's popped. It's fun to hear corn grains explode as they heat up.

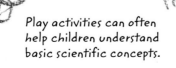

Play activities can often help children understand basic scientific concepts.

Safety point

Supervise children at all times in the kitchen and when they are playing with water.

Let's think about it

A young child's brain develops at an incredibly rapid rate, and what they can do, learn and understand develops quickly, too. Experts emphasize that children achieve far more in later life if you let them learn things through play, in a relaxed way, when they are young. These pages focus on games and puzzles that help develop a child's concentration and thinking skills.

Do you remember?

Children's memories improve enormously during these years. They may tell you what they wore to a party, what they did at preschool that morning, or remind you that you'd promised pizza, not pasta, for lunch. On the left and below there are some suggestions for activities that allow them to see what they can remember.

Memory games

• Say 'I went shopping and I bought an apple', for example. Ask a child to repeat what you said, and add to it — 'I went shopping and bought an apple and a cake'. Then you add a third thing to the list, and so on.

• Help children memorize a rhyme, or tongue twister. (There are some ideas on the Usborne Quicklinks Website — see page 120). If they keep repeating it, a chunk at a time, they'll learn it. If they get stuck, give them a clue to help, not the whole answer.

Useful tip

Memory games are good for confidence-building. The more children remember successfully, the more they feel they can do.

1. Put up to ten small objects on a tray. Tell children to have a really good look, then cover it with a cloth.

2. Take the tray away, remove one of the objects, then cover the tray up again with the cloth.

3. Can children spot what's missing when you take the cloth away? Give them a clue if they're stuck.

Time to think

Many people caring for young children are amazed to see them really concentrating and figuring things out for themselves. Most will spend time happily absorbed in building with blocks, fitting puzzles together or threading big beads onto string. On the right are some more activities that focus on helping children learn to think.

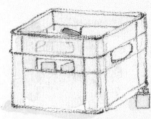

Thinking activities

• Start a collection of blocks, rail-tracks or construction kits that can be added to. Ones that can be played with in several ways are best.

• Jigsaw puzzles help children learn how things do or don't fit together, and improve their concentration.

• Ask for a child's help to solve problems. How should you arrange fruit in a bowl or line up some of their toys on a shelf?

• Cut pictures out of a young children's comic (or draw some yourself). Can a child put them in the right order to make a story?

It's my turn

By around four years old, many children are doing more with other children, solving problems together. There may be a few arguments, but remember that they need practice to develop their social skills and learn to cooperate with each other. Let them play some simple board games and card games for young children. Some will require them to count while others need them to match pictures, which are both early math skills.

Playing card games and board games with friends helps children develop their social skills.

Children usually enjoy figuring out how things fit together.

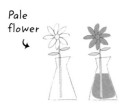

Pale flower

Color power

Fill a vase or bottle with cold water. Add some drops of food coloring. Put the stalk of a pale flower into the vase. Over a few hours, the flower should change color.

Floating boats

Help a child mold some aluminum foil into a basic boat shape. Fill a bowl with water and see how well the boat floats. Now count how many small coins you can put into the boat before it sinks.

Fizzy ice

Put some ice cubes into a tall glass. Let children sprinkle on some salt and listen to the sound the ice makes as it melts. Don't let them drink any of the salty water, though.

Let's find out

One of the best ways of helping young children learn things is to let them find them out for themselves. These easy experiments show them some simple science in action. They can all be done at home, using everyday things, but children will need your help to set them up and get the most from them.

Look behind you

Young children usually find mirrors fascinating. When they are standing in front of a big one, help them to understand that mirrors show opposites – if they lift one arm up, it looks like the other one in the mirror reflection. You could also let them try using a magnifying mirror to get a close-up look at themselves. Many pharmacies sell these mirrors for shaving or makeup.

Children like being able to see the back of their heads if you hold up one mirror while they look into another.

The screen scene

If young children are watching television, it's an opportunity for you to cook a meal, feed the baby or just sit down – television can really help you, but it has disadvantages for children too. This section of the book looks at how to get the best out of children's television, DVDs and computer games. It also outlines some of the worries experts have about them. As usual, try to strive for a good balance.

Watch and learn

Suitable television programs or DVDs give children great pleasure.

Young children need some quieter activities in their busy day.

Many programs and games are educationally valuable.

Favorite programs or DVDs are comforting and familiar.

Things children enjoy watching can lead to other games and activities.

Disadvantages of television

• If children are watching television they are not playing, talking or being active, or learning to communicate and interact with others.

• Research shows that some children are less sociable if they watch a lot of television.

• Commercials can influence how your child perceives the world, and can lead to children pestering you for things you'd prefer not to buy.

• Children seem to know that cartoon violence is not real but many still copy it in games.

• Young children can worry about sad, scary things they watch, and become fearful.

• The attitudes shown on some programs may not be ones you want a child to copy.

If you can, watch television with your children so you can see how they react to programs and talk about them together afterward.

What should we watch?

The advantages of young children watching television are listed on the previous page. It is a tricky area, though, and studies show it's vital to know what, and how much, children watch. These pages can help you decide what role, if any, you want television to play in your home.

What's bad about television?

The disadvantages of children watching television are listed on the left, but if you follow the guidelines on these pages, television shouldn't have a negative impact on your child.

There's a lot of debate about whether watching violence on television makes children behave aggressively. Firstly, children should never watch violent adult programs, but some people feel that even cartoons show too much fighting. If you want to discourage children from copying it, just don't let them watch these programs. It may make no difference, but you are the best judge of the effect any program may be having on a child: talk to them and then stop them from watching if you are worried.

What to watch

Some families choose not to have a television, which has the advantage of allowing more time for play, talking together and other activities. However, it can lead to children being left out of games and conversations with television-watching friends, which is not ideal. Here are some suggestions for achieving a balance in what gets watched and for how long:

You could make a note of when good children's programs are on, so your family learns to choose what to watch.

• Show that television is fine from time to time, but it shouldn't be on so much it keeps anyone from talking, or playing.

• Set a limit for total 'screen time' each day. This includes using computers for games and activities as well as watching television.

• Don't let children have a television in their bedrooms. They could see unsuitable programs without your even knowing it.

Experts believe that no young child should be in front of any screen for more than two hours a day in total.

Useful tip

If you have, or can borrow, a camcorder, young children will enjoy watching themselves on television — and you probably will, too.

Familiar friends

Most young children enjoy watching familiar movies or shows again and again. They may well become completely engrossed in the stories, or pretend they are a character in a movie. This is all natural.

The same guidelines apply to DVDs and videos as for television: make sure children only watch movies suitable for their age, try to watch DVDs with them, and don't let them watch anything for too long.

Seeing movies that are unsuitable for their age-group can make children scared and anxious.

Mouse time

For many children, computers are just another part of childhood, and they are completely at ease using them. The vast majority of schools have computers, and many children play on them at home, too. The lists on the left show what's good, and what's not so good, about letting young children use them.

Young children are so quick to learn that they can benefit in many ways from computers. You do need to make sure you always know what they are doing on them, however. At home, make sure you install Parental Controls to any computer with internet access. It's important that children play age-appropriate computer games, and you continue to interact with them about the games they are playing.

Computer benefits:

• Children can find out about things that interest them by learning how to use search engines and find websites.

• Many interactive games help children develop logic, problem-solving, creative and artistic skills.

• Playing on a computer with other children teaches them to cooperate, take turns and follow instructions.

Disadvantages:

• Playing on a computer does not give children any opportunities to be physically active.

• It's better to avoid any 'war-type' games. Young children may get confused, or even scared, by them.

• Playing alone does not develop children's social skills. Make sure they play with others as often as possible.

Teach children not to lie on the floor or slouch in their chairs when using the computer.

Are you sitting comfortably?

Though they may prefer to lie on the floor, it's worth making sure your child sits comfortably at a computer for most of the time they are playing on it. Make sure the chair is at the right height, that they can see the screen and reach the mouse easily.

Don't let using computers replace books, balls or board games. Make sure it's just one of the activities a child does.

Trips and traveling

Most young children get excited about going on a trip, as they are always eager to do and see something different. This section has guidelines on taking young children out, ideas on where to take them and tips on how to try to make sure that any trip you go on together is a success.

Getting out

It's worth making the effort to go out — a change in routine is good for all of you from time to time.

Children see, and learn, lots of new things every time they go out, however simple the outing.

A trip out together can be an especially memorable time for you and a young child.

Children need to learn about how to behave in different places and with different people.

Being out takes you away from your chores, giving you time to concentrate on your child and just enjoy some time together.

Everyday outings

• For a child, a trip to a park is often more fun than staying at home. If the weather is good, take a picnic and let them try out all the play equipment.

• Take a trip on a bus, train or ferry. Let your child ask for the tickets, and hand over the money. A journey gives them plenty of things to see and people to watch.

• If you have a river nearby, children will be fascinated by the comings and goings. You could watch planes take off and land, too.

Where should we go today?

Children enjoy variety – even the simplest of outings gives them plenty to see and ask questions about. When you are out, try to remember that small children's behavior is often unpredictable, however much trouble you've taken. If they misbehave, deal with it, then forget it. If you accept that the day may have its ups and downs, you'll probably both enjoy it more.

Young children can be entertained by seeing a car wash in action, or watching the bulldozers at a building site for a while. On the left are some more suggestions for some easy outings. Libraries, local papers and websites are also good places to find out about events happening near you.

Before you go

It's a good idea to do some preparation before going out with a young child. Talk to them about where you are going in advance as this helps them feel involved, and lets them know what to expect. Go online and find out about sharks, if you are going to an aquarium, for example. If you're going to be gone awhile, pack some food and drinks and something for them to do if there is a long drive.

Don't forget to involve your child in getting everything ready for your day out.

Useful tip

Children can't concentrate for long, and may get tired. Remember to take things at their pace on trips, not yours, and don't expect too much of them.

Special trips

On the right are some ideas for special trips, which may be further from home. If you can look at the website of the attraction you are going to before your visit, you can see what's on offer for young children and plan your day accordingly. Many of these kinds of places have a gift and souvenir shop, but as young children usually have no awareness of cost, it might be an idea to set a clear price limit if you choose to venture inside.

Give some basic rules for when you are out. Children must listen to you, and hold your hand, for example.

A visit to a farm to see some animals is a big treat for most young children.

Special outings

• Family game centers often have ball pits, inflatable jumping structures and lots of other games. Make sure they have plenty to drink and just let them play.

• Many museums have interactive exhibits, art activities and special events to interest young children.

• A day trip to the beach, a forest, a historic building or a busy harbor gives young children things to talk about for weeks, and remember for much longer.

• A trip to a wildlife park or zoo is an exciting event and provides lots of new things to find out about.

Show and tell

When you get home, let children talk about what they saw and did, look at photos, or call someone such as a grandparent to tell them all about it. Retelling the story of their day makes it even more memorable for them, and you may be surprised by the things they remember.

Story
CDs

• Songs and stories on tape or CD may drive you nuts, but entertain children. Head-phones may be a good idea.

• You could buy some books or cards with ideas for travel games for young children to play on trips.

Are we there yet?

Car travel is part of everyday life for most children, but long rides in particular can be tricky, as children can become bored and misbehave. If a child is really acting up on a long car ride, it's safer to stop and calm them down, or their distress may affect your concentration. This page has tips and ideas for making car rides more enjoyable for children, which makes traveling less stressful for everyone.

First of all, you might consider which methods of travel you have available to you for longer trips. If you use an unfamiliar method, your child enjoy the new experience. You may be able to go by plane, bus, taxi, ferry, train or subway rather than driving yourself. Children have more freedom to move about, can draw and do games more easily and see the scenery better.

Children who don't get travel sick might enjoy having a large, firm drawing pad and some crayons to draw with.

If you're driving, stop regularly, for everyone to get some air, and use the bathroom.

Give children small snacks during the journey.

• Play 'spot a red car', or 'a white bus'. Older children could keep count of the total you spot on the trip.

• Start a simple story (try 'One sunny day, Ben had to go on a trip...') and take turns adding the next part of it.

• See if older children can spot and count road signs that match one that you point out to them.

Time to celebrate

Whether it's a special birthday party, a
wedding, Halloween, or a big religious
holiday, most young children love the
build-up to a celebration and enjoy being
involved on the day, so it's a good idea
to include them in the preparations and
festivities as much as you can.

Days to remember

By marking 'special days' young children learn the important
holidays and traditions in your family year, and how
they are celebrated.

Most children enjoy new experiences, such as eating
different food and dressing in special clothes.

Lots of games, stories and activities can stem
from festivals and celebrations.

Celebrating special days helps children feel part of
the group of people who care about them.

Religious holidays and festivals give an ideal opportunity
to talk to children about how other people celebrate
important occasions.

Party time

Most young children consider their birthday to be the most important day of the year, and they will probably want a party to celebrate. Organizing a party for young children can be expensive and stressful, but these pages have some tips to try to make sure everyone has a good time.

When, where and how many?

One of the first things to think about when planning a young child's party is how many guests to invite. Many children are more comfortable with fewer people, rather than a big crowd, so it's fine just to invite a few close friends if that feels right. Here are some other things to consider:

It might be best to delay present opening until later in the party. Don't forget to make a note of who gave what.

If you're going to serve food, try to offer it near a normal mealtime.

• Will you have the party on your child's birthday, or keep the day for a family celebration? A weekend is often more convenient for a party.

• A park is an inexpensive place to have a party. If the weather is bad, why not rent out a room at a family game or community center?

• If you opt for a bigger party, were any of the child's friends born around the same date? A joint party can help to spread the cost.

Useful tip
Party bags can add a lot to the cost — just fill them with a balloon, a small chocolate bar and a pot of bubble solution.

Games to play

If you hold a party at a family entertainment center, the staff may organize the games for you. If you're doing it all yourself, make sure other adults help you with the games, food, bathroom trips and 'guest control'. If the children are going to play games, it's a nice idea to have small prizes to hand out. Children this age sometimes find it hard to lose, so you might want to have a few extra prizes on hand.

On the right are some games you could try. There are more on Usborne Quicklinks (see page 120). It's best to do more energetic games before the food, and quieter ones afterward. Avoid any that are hard to explain or need lots of props and don't forget to take some music and a player if necessary.

Biggest isn't always best

It's easy to feel pressured into holding an elaborate party for your child, but an afternoon with a few friends, some streamers and a cake is probably all that's needed to make the day feel special. Try to remember that the birthday is the focus of the occasion, not the extravagance of the party.

Pin the tail on the donkey:

1. Draw a donkey outline on a large sheet of paper and cut out a tail shape from cardboard.

2. Blindfold each child in turn and help them attach the tail on the paper with tape or poster putty.

3. Mark where each child puts the tail with their name; the nearest guess wins a prize.

Musical chairs:

Children have to sit down on a chair when the music stops. The last one to sit down is out.

Musical statues:

Children have to 'freeze' when the music stops. Anyone seen moving is out.

You could have the children play a variety of simple games like 'duck, duck, goose', musical chairs, 'red light, green light' or include quieter activities like face painting or sidewalk chalks.

Holidays and religious festivals

Your family may celebrate several holidays or festivals a year, or maybe you just mark a few traditional celebrations and birthdays, weddings and anniversaries. Whatever the occasion, children usually enjoy special events and the customs surrounding them. Here are some ideas for making the most of celebrations with young children.

Everyone's different

Many children will learn about some of the holidays and festivals that different cultures celebrate in preschool or kindergarten. If you don't feel you know enough to tell children about beliefs and customs different from your own, you'll find some information on the Usborne Quicklinks Website (see page 120). Each festival is different, but many involve special food, special clothes, giving gifts and getting friends and family together. On the left are some ways of helping children be a part of any holidays or festivals your family celebrates.

Most children enjoy dressing up and playing games, whatever the occasion.

Getting children involved

• Explain what the holiday or festival means, or its history. If you aren't sure, find out from books, or the internet.

• Let children help with any preparations such as putting up decorations or buying special candles.

• Let them help you buy gifts, so they can see it's about giving, as well as receiving.

• Will children need to wear special clothes for the day? If they do, show them how to get these clothes ready.

Before, during and after

Although most young children enjoy days that are very different from their normal routine, some can become overwhelmed, and sometimes misbehave. To help make sure everyone has a good time and head off any upsets, try following these steps:

1. Talk about what is going to happen in advance. Children will feel involved, know what to expect and how long it might last.

2. Get help with the cooking or other chores, so you can make time for children during the celebration.

3. Talk about the day afterward, and thank your child for helping. Which part of the day did they like best?

Children could help make some special food for a celebration.

Less can be more

Some festivals involve a lot of extra work and expense for adults. Afterward some people may feel disappointed, as all the work did not produce as much enjoyment as they had hoped for, and the children are now complaining of boredom. Overall, remember that family celebrations are often among our strongest memories of childhood, both good and bad. They are more likely to be special if you keep the focus on spending time with people you care about, rather than worrying too much about elaborate food and presents.

• Children could draw or make simple presents for the family. Explain that the time they put in is part of the gift.

• Make sure there are simple things to enjoy, such as party hats, homemade name cards on the table, or funny games.

• After the event, you could help children make 'thank you' cards or notes for people who have given them presents.

Making simple decorations, costumes, cards or masks helps children feel really involved in the festivities.

Always try to talk to your child about what is going to happen, reassuring them that you will still love them just as much.

If things are difficult, it may help to talk to a health professional about your feelings, and your child's behavior.

Tears and tantrums

Most young children will have regular explosions of temper, or tantrums, long after toddlerhood and it can be especially hard to cope with such behavior if you are feeling stressed or under pressure in some way.

Children are very sensitive to change and their behavior often worsens after a new baby arrives, or they move to a new house or begin preschool or day care. Guiding children through other big changes such as divorce or separation can be especially hard, as they may only feel able to show their feelings through tantrums, or not eating and sleeping well. These may be difficult times for both of you, but you need to remind yourself they will eventually pass.

Try to accept that children may be angry, sad, or both, from time to time. It's better that they show it than bottle it up.

Bad manners

Unfortunately, young children often reserve their worst behavior for times when you really want to be proud of them. They seem to realize how important it is that they 'sit and eat politely' – and refuse to do either. Here are some tactics to try to prevent or deal with this behavior.

Most children do learn how to control their behavior, but it can be a very gradual process.

- If you are visiting someone or going to a restaurant, take things to distract your child. Try crayons and a notebook.

- Take some healthy snacks, too, in case you have to wait to eat. Hungry children are even more likely to misbehave.

- If things get out of hand, take them outside. There is nothing worse than having to discipline a child in public.

114

Useful information

This final part of the book has more
information that you might find useful
as a parent or caregiver. There is such a huge
amount of material available about all aspects
of caring for children – on the internet, in
books, magazines, and so on – that it can feel
overwhelming, so try using these suggestions
as a starting point.

What will I find here?

Guidelines for caring for children with special
needs, and sources of support.

Basic first-aid advice for everyday children's
injuries and minor accidents.

Information about useful websites to visit.

Development charts so you can see at a glance
what most children can do at certain ages.

Special needs

Play is the main method of learning for young children of all abilities and ages and many of the activities described in this book can be enjoyed by children with special needs. Some of the activities may just need adapting a little and on the right are some general points to remember when deciding what to play. Some web resources, sources of information and online activities for children with specific special needs are described on the facing page.

Every child is special

When you care for a child with special needs at home, one of the many skills you develop is the ability to understand what your child likes to do and how they feel, in lots of different situations. This takes time, patience and a great deal of sensitivity, but it means you can usually tell which games and activities your child will enjoy, and which they may find tricky, or frustrating. Don't forget to pass what you learn on to your child's caregivers, and to their teachers when your child starts school.

Most experts now believe that children with special needs should be included in mainstream education wherever possible. Many children will need extra help, but all the children gain a lot from playing and learning together.

Most children, whatever their needs, enjoy playing with others.

Things to remember

You need to plan things carefully when setting up play opportunities for children with special needs. Here are a few things to remember:

• Some children with special needs may take longer than other children to do a puzzle, or fit a track together. Be patient, and give them extra help if they need it.

• If toys, books or paper might slip out of reach of less mobile children, you could stick them to the floor or table with poster putty, masking tape or Velcro™.

• Try to avoid a child with special needs becoming isolated in any way. Make sure wheelchair users sit near other children, for instance.

• Every child is unique and deserves the opportunity to develop and explore. Really trying to understand the way they see the world is vital.

Getting support

Taking care of a child with special needs is very hard work. There are lots of groups and organizations that offer support and enable parents and caregivers to learn from each other's experiences. Ask healthcare professionals how to contact both national and local groups, or go to **www.usborne-quicklinks.com** and type in the keywords 'entertain children' for links to specific sites.

Web resources

A number of websites offer activities for children with special needs. You can find links to those below on the Usborne Quicklinks Website:

CBeebies website has a wide range of activities for children with special needs, including stories, songs, games, counting and music-making activities. Some activities have been modified for children to play using only the keyboard, or switches (devices that let children access a computer when their disabilities prevent them using a mouse).

The content specifically designed for children with special needs includes activities for children on the autistic spectrum; blind and visually impaired children; children who are deaf or hard of hearing; dyslexic children; children with learning difficulties; children with physical difficulties, and children with speech and language disorders.

In the 'Grownups' part of this website, you can find out more about this content and about devices that can help children with special needs use computers. You can also read about other parents' and caregivers' experiences.

PBS Parents website has a great number of resources for the parents and caregivers of children with learning disabilities. It includes advice on recognizing and understanding potential problems, and strategies and tips for helping and supporting children at home and school.

SEN Teacher website allows you to access a huge range of resources and activities for children with special needs. The resources include free software, video clips, printable activities and switch games. The site covers blindness and visual impairment, dyspraxia, dyslexia, SPLD (semantic pragmatic language disorder), epilepsy, Down's syndrome, speech and language disorders, ASD (autistic spectrum disorder), autism and Asperger's syndrome. There are also links to current news items about special needs.

KidNeeds website aims to give parents, caregivers and children with special needs access to a comprehensive range of information and resources worldwide. It includes information about children's mental health problems.

Access to suitable toys and books is especially important for a child with special needs.

Everyday injuries

Young children are likely to have plenty of bumps and bruises and be sick from time to time. Here's how to deal with some common childhood mishaps and illnesses. If you are ever really worried about a child's health, contact your doctor right away.

Minor cuts and scrapes

Children cut or scrape themselves alarmingly regularly. If the wound is on the head, or won't stop bleeding, get medical help.

1. Comfort the child, wash your hands, and sit them down comfortably somewhere.

2. Gently wash the cut under running water. Pat dry and cover with some sterile gauze.

3. Raise the injured area and clean around it. If the wound is still bleeding, press on it firmly.

4. Remove the gauze and cover the cut with a dressing or adhesive bandage bigger than the cut itself.

A few soothing words and a bandage may be all that's needed.

Sunburn

Young children burn very quickly in hot sun. Use a good children's sunscreen and reapply it regularly, especially after they have been in water. Make sure they wear a hat; one with a flap that also shades the back of their neck is ideal. If a child's skin does get red and sore from over-exposure to the sun, cool the affected area with a damp sponge, apply aftersun or calamine lotion and offer plenty of cool drinks. If a child's skin blisters, go to the doctor.

Sun hats help children stay cool as well as keeping the sun off.

Burns and scalds

Young children have delicate skin that burns easily. This is what to do if your child gets burned or scalded.

1. Take a burned or scalded child away from the problem. Hold wherever is burned under cold running water for at least 10 minutes.

2. Take any clothes around the area off, cutting them if necessary, but don't try to remove fabric stuck to the burned or scalded skin.

3. Once cool, loosely cover the area with a sterile dressing. Call an ambulance or take the child to the hospital.

Useful tip

Some children are allergic to adhesive bandages, which cause a rash. Sterile dressings are a good alternative.

Bumps and bruises

Young children are so active that they often get bumps and bruises. Usually, a cuddle, raising the hurt area, and keeping a cool, wet pad on it for five minutes will be enough treatment. If the bump is on the head, however, you need to keep a close eye on the child for the next 24 hours. If they become drowsy, are sick or say they can't see properly, go straight to the Emergency room, as they may have concussion.

Fever

Young children who feel hot and clammy to the touch, have a blank look in their eyes and seem miserable may have a high temperature. Check it with a thermometer; a normal temperature is 36–37.5°C (97–99°F). If it's higher than this, follow the steps below.

There are many different instruments that can be used to take a child's temperature. Use the one you feel most comfortable with.

1. If your doctor advises, follow the directions on the package and give your child the correct dosage of child-strength acetaminophen.

2. Put the child somewhere cool and offer them plenty of cool drinks.

3. Sponge their body with washcloths dipped in tepid water and squeezed out.

4. If the child's temperature stays high, they develop a rash of purple spots, or you are still worried, seek medical help right away.

Choking

It is very frightening when a child has something stuck in their throat and cannot breathe. If they can't cough the object out, you need to stay calm and act fast:

1. Bend the child forward and give up to five sharp blows between the shoulder blades using the heel of your hand. Check their mouth.

2. If choking continues, stand or kneel behind the child and wrap your arms around the top half of their body.

3. Place one of your fists between their belly button and the bottom of their breastbone, and hold on to it with your other hand.

4. Pull the fist upward and inward sharply up to five times, but do not use too much force.

5. Check the child's mouth after each of these abdominal thrusts to see if it's clear. If the child is still choking after three cycles of back blows and thrusts, get help immediately.

6. Always take a child who has had abdominal thrusts to a doctor to be checked afterward.

Insect bites and stings

Occasionally, children may get stung or bitten by insects. Try to remove a visible stinger, by scraping it sideways with your nail. Apply ice for insect bites and stings to reduce the swelling. Call a doctor immediately if the child has any adverse reactions or the puncture isn't healing well.

Taking care of sick children

Taking care of a sick child is tiring. If they have to go to the hospital, you will need to be with them to offer support and comfort. Accept offers of help from family and friends to give you a break.

Further help

Caring for young children is very demanding. There is no shortage of experts offering advice, and it can be easy to feel you have to be perfect (and have failed if you're not). These pages have some suggestions for where to look for useful help and information.

You are not alone

Many people who care for young children feel lonely at times. It can be especially hard when children start at preschool or kindergarten, as you may suddenly feel isolated, perhaps without anything to replace the sociable toddler groups, or the daily demands of a small child – particularly if you are not working. It's a new phase for both of you.

Try to meet the other preschool or kindergarten parents if you can, or go to any events the school holds. Everyone there has young children in their lives, even if their work or home situation is different from yours.

Internet links

The internet is a good source of information for parents and caregivers. At the Usborne Quicklinks Website there are links to lots of useful websites and things to download such as templates and coloring sheets. To visit the sites, go to **www.usborne-quicklinks.com** and type the keywords 'entertain children'. These are some things you can find:

- Art activities to print out and try, such as templates for masks.

- A selection of good online games suitable for young children.

- Information about different holidays and religions around the world.

- Websites that support the families of children with special needs.

- Songs, rhymes and party games for young children to play.

Internet safety

Please note that the websites recommended on Usborne Quicklinks are regularly reviewed, but the content of a website may change and Usborne Publishing is not responsible for the content or availability of websites other than its own.

Starting school

As well as the activities described in this book, there are many ways you can help prepare your child for school and make the transition easier for everybody. It helps if children know what to expect, so talk to them as much as possible about things that happen at school. On a practical level, try to make sure your child can put on their own shoes and coat, get dressed by themselves, go to the bathroom and wash their hands, knows how to hold a pencil correctly and can use silverware.

Knowing a little about what to expect at school can help children settle in.

For many young children, starting school is an exciting time, and a chance to make lots of new friends. Others find it harder to settle in, so it's very important that you keep in close contact with staff at the school and talk about how things are going. If your child is finding it hard to get used to their new routine, make sure everyone who cares for them knows how the child is feeling so they can help you both overcome these problems.

Development charts

The charts on the following two pages describe some of the main things most children can do at certain ages. They will enable you to judge how much help children might need as you do various activities together. The information covers children's development from the age of two and a half to five in the four areas outlined below.

Always remember, though, that every child is different and children develop at different rates so very few will do everything exactly as is described in these charts. Also, although it's natural for parents and caregivers to compare notes, try not to take too much notice of what other children can do, or when they can do it. If you have any genuine worries about your child's development, it's always best to talk to your child's doctor.

Movement skills
This is about what children's bodies can do.

Hand-eye coordination
This covers what they can do with their hands and fingers.

Language development
This is about what they can hear, say and understand.

Emotional development
This is about how they relate to caregivers and other children.

2½ – 3 years

Movement: Children run confidently, climb furniture and play apparatus and walk up and down stairs, usually putting both feet on each step while holding onto a rail. Growing physical coordination.

Hand-eye coordination: Children can hold a pencil in the hand they will probably write with and make marks with it.

Language: Children know over 200 recognizable words and talk a great deal (though with lots of errors). They are likely to ask lots of 'Who?' and 'What?' questions, talk to themselves while playing and know some songs and rhymes.

Emotional development: Children are likely to have tantrums, and are still very dependent on adults. They may still find it hard to share with others.

3 – 3½ years

Movement: Children are confident on stairs and may jump 'feet together' from the bottom one. They can climb up most climbing structures confidently, ride a tricycle using the pedals, and can steer it too.

Hand-eye coordination: Children can throw and catch a large, soft ball, cut with child's scissors and build a tower of up to ten building blocks. They will also be able to eat with a fork and a spoon.

Language: Children talk a great deal and their speech will be understandable to more people. They enjoy hearing stories – often the same ones, repeatedly.

Emotional development: Children will often be very loving and affectionate. They'll like to help with chores and play make-believe games with others.

3½ – 4 years

Movement: Children will be growing in confidence in climbing, jumping and hopping. They can walk and run on tiptoe; bounce, throw, kick and catch balls.

Hand-eye coordination: Children are able to hold a pencil with good control and pick up small objects such as short pieces of thread. Their drawings of people may now have a head, legs, and body – and sometimes hands.

Language: Children's speech will be much more correct and easy to understand. They'll like hearing and telling stories and relating everyday experiences.

Emotional development: Children will be more caring toward others, and get upset if others are. They may be strong-willed with playmates and adults; lively, curious and imaginative, and increasingly able to dress themselves.

4 – 5 years

Movement: Children will be very agile and willing to take risks. They can hop easily, use a swing independently and play ball games with bats, rules and goals.

Hand-eye coordination: Children can pick up tiny objects, such as crumbs. They can draw the outline, and perhaps some details, of a house; faces with more features and hands that may have fingers. They may write a few letters.

Language: Children will ask lots of 'Why?', 'When?' and 'How?' questions. They know and can count up to 20 or more, and enjoy acting out stories.

Emotional development: Children understand the idea of taking turns and sharing. They can dress themselves, make their own friends and are usually very caring toward others, and animals. They are now more independent.

Index

With thanks to...

Bethan, Rhiannon, Mari and Geoff; Molly and friends, and
all the staff, parents and children at Cannons Health Club Nursery,
Surbiton; Long Ditton Infant and Nursery School; Long Ditton
St Mary's School; Lower Roundhurst Farm, West Sussex; Olivia Brooks
for the 'Kandinsky' and 'Seurat' pictures on page 17; Janey Harold
for the 'Chart about me' on page 64; Claire Masset for
additional picture and website research.

Photo credits:

The publishers are grateful to the following for permission to reproduce material:
p10 © Masterfile Corporation; p29 © Design Pics Inc./Alamy; p36 © Westend 61/
Alamy; p42 © Peter Beavis/Getty Images; p60 © Chris Windsor/Getty Images;
p72 © Darren Baker/Alamy; p84 © Daniella Boutin

Additional consultants: Alison Bell (swimming)
and Dawn Upton, St. John Ambulance (first aid)

Additional illustrations: Dubravka Kolanovic

Digital imaging: Keith Furnival